The
Wonder  of it All

The
Wonder of it All

By: Roger A. Goodman

Order this book online at www.trafford.com
or email orders@trafford.com

Most Trafford titles are also available at major online book retailers.

Printed in the United States of America.

ISBN: 978-1-4269-2318-0 (sc)
ISBN: 978-1-4269-2319-7 (hc)
ISBN: 978-1-4269-7884-5 (e)

Library of Congress Control Number: 2009914035

Trafford rev. 12/07/2011

 www.trafford.com

North America & International
toll-free: 1 888 232 4444 (USA & Canada)
phone: 250 383 6864 ✦ fax: 812 355 4082

FREE AS AN EAGLE TO PRAISE GOD

God discovers each of us many times in strange, mysterious and different ways. He found me battling chronic depression for many years. The journey was filled with many disappointments and dead-end searches. From God's rejection to acceptance. From confusion to delusion to confession. From anger to love. From lack of trust to trust. From misconceptions to truth. From hurts to forgiveness. From an impatient heart to a more understanding heart. From God's nature to a sensitivity for God's creative genius and Jesus Christ's redemptive grace. To listening to "God's Whispering Hope."

THE WINDS OF THE SPIRIT

From a Sunday church service program

The winds of the spirit have given us breath and the fire of the spirit has kindled in us a love for God and each other. We open our lives to the presence of God and trust God's promise to us that we can live new lives of freedom and grace. May God help us to be true people of the spirit, letting holy surprises fill our days.

Is God's invisibility and silent voice reduced to words on paper? Not if we open the window to "The Wonder of it All!" God does not live in a book or a box, he lives in our hearts and souls.

DEDICATION

A very special "Thank you" to my wife of forty eight years who walked beside me during my struggles with God and other ordeals of life. She put purpose and meaning in our life as we walked and talked together in a loving relationship. I thank her for her patience, understanding and encouragement as I gradually step by step rendered the thoughts here in disclosed. As a father of my daughters Cheryl, Wendy and Brenda I was not a good Christian leader. Circumstances of life interfered with that responsibility. I ask for their forgiveness. I love them dearly. I wrote this book with them in my heart. May it be beneficial to them in the years ahead in terms of establishing a positive and fruitful relationship with their Lord, Jesus Christ. If it is deemed appropriate and worthy for my grandchildren, please allow them to inherit the fruits of this labor. May you progress onward with Jesus Christ our Lord at the helm

With love, Dad, 2009

ACKNOWLEDGMENTS

I will avoid specifically recognizing one or more people, for this book is a composite of thoughts by me, Pastors, friends, hymnists and authors of Christian books. I am sincerely grateful for their knowledge and insights. A special thank you goes to the English teacher who proofread the manuscript correcting numerous grammatical errors. All of it afforded me the opportunity and privilege of bringing awareness to God's creative genius and Christ's redemptive grace as seen through the window of "The Wonder of it"

WHERE IS THE MONEY GOING ?

Any monies generated by the sale of this book will go into a registered bank account fund designated for the Katrina and Ike hurricane victims. It will be distributed among churches in that region of the country to help members who need financial assistance to get back into their homes and get emotionally back on their feet. Christ tells us to foster goodwill. Donations will be honored according to screened interviews and submitted applications. This will be supervised by trustees to validate the process so that it is not misused.

TABLE OF CONTENTS

WHY THIS BOOK

Life is like a storybook,
an endless flowing brook.
Continuous flow through the seasons
only God knows the reasons.
Youth, adulthood and old age,
daily turning the page.
We journey on our way,
counting our blessings each day,

We know not where the stream leads,
often obstacles will impede.
Troubles of life cast a shadow,
joy departs like a fleeting sparrow.
Yet, behind the cloud is the hope of tomorrow,
rays of hope, even when bad winds blow.
There behind the cloud lies,
the source of our strength to realize.
Following God's lead,
the answer to our needs.
Brook....to river....to seashore,
onward travel, discovering more.
Endless waves washing ashore.
God's grace blessing us evermore.

Now these words I present to you,
of god's promise ever true.
Why this book ? You should ask,
poems written for a special task.
Thoughts of God in poetic verse,
revealed through this book as you traverse.
Although I am old,
there is a story to be told.
As these poems unfold,
God's grace behold.
This book is my mission,

surely, God bestows permission.
I am old, yet, I have a goal,
to reach another soul.
Another hill to climb,
"Unto The Hills" while there is time.

A pinnacle to reach,
my poems do teach.
Poems for good cheer,
as to the future you peer.
To open thine eyes to see,
the assurance offered to thee.
I hope you will understand,
reading with book in hand.
Of thoughts found in quietude,
these words tell the magnitude.
With you these thoughts I share,
knowing that Christ really cares.
These poems make us aware,
that he is always there.
It is the knowing,
that fills our hearts overflowing.
Know of God's Good Grace,
our leader of the human race.
It gives us the strength to face,
life with hope and a smiling face.

                                        RG

"Commit your works to the Lord, and your thoughts will be
              established." (Proverbs 16:3,KJ)
"But the manifestation of the Spirit is given to each one for
          the profit of all." (1 Cor. 12:7,KJ)
    "There are diversities of gifts, but the same Spirit."
                    (1 Cor. 12:4,KJ)

PREFACE

WHY THIS BOOK

Generally speaking this book is the story of a teenage boy who struggled with the invisibility of God well into his adulthood. This book is a display of how he coped with that dilemma in his life. By reading scripture, writing essays and poems plus designing colorful stained glass work he discovered to a much greater degree the mysteries surrounding the spirit of God, the author of our life. The chapters that follow reveals how he grew spiritually (faith) by exploring God's wonders.

There came a time in my life when I marveled at what God had given us. As time went on it had a profound impact on my walk into faith. It became a compelling force to open the door to a new spiritual frame of mind. There began a journey into "The Wonder of it All." Thus, the title of this book. By delving into that realm of thinking, I hoped to discover more thoroughly the image of God, the parameters of Christianity, my significance in our Lord and the prerequisites for salvation. The title of the song "I Believe" prompted my search to confirm with greater understanding and conviction the question "Why I should believe?" "What is on the other side of salvation?" Therefore, redemption became an issue of relative importance. Before we approach Jesus Christ we must be absolutely certain of our spiritual reasons for entering into a covenant with our Lord. The binding of that agreement is essential to Christ as well as for ourselves.

The writing of this book has been a major turning point in my life, moving from spiritual negativism, to depression, to hope and to greater understanding. All the result of looking through the window of "The Wonder of it all", therein discovering God's creative genius and Christ's redemptive grace. This attitude underscores the great adventure of mental and spiritual freedom to explore the gifts of God. Where a more confirmed faith and trust results from the search. Where a confused faith grows to one that emerges with greater confidence to grasp the full meaning of Christianity. The adventure of writing this book took me into uncharted waters. The emotions were like riding a roller coaster. Relationships waned and swayed. The past faded into obscurity and ushered in a future filled with hope. The spirit to live today and tomorrow dwells with in, hopefully, steadfast until Christ calls me home.

This experience produced a calling to write, to design, to fabricate, and tell of this adventure. Thousands of you could be doing the same thing, for each of us have a story to tell. My personal objective is to reveal how a man coped with depression and the invisible Ghost in our lives. By sharing this story, perhaps, it might restore other people who are experiencing the same dilemma. Hopefully, God looks on with approval. The book has been taken to Him in prayer and He knows the reasons, for He has prevailed in this search. Each step of the way there were new discoveries. Any words written or designs fabricated relative to this mission are shallow in the eyes of God. It is a speck in a thimble. I am unworthy. Yet, we as Christians are on assignment by God to bear fruit and spread the message of how Christ inspires our lives. I have been given the motivation and inspiration to do these things. It is a response to a force propelling the interest and desire. God says; praise Him with any offering you have and He will be pleased, whether it be big or small, a fortune or a penny, small words or lots of words. So long as it is worthy and honest in His eyes, I will hear your supplications. Most of all He wants our soul to prepare it for eternity. For it is in Christ that you will find strength and rest. What we have to offer is a measure of our faith. Like the eagle, we are free to praise the Lord and give Him the glory. Jesus said, "Man shall not live by bread alone, but by every word that proceeds from the mouth of God." (Matt. 4:4, KJ) It is the spirit of God that induces the spirit to transform us into a new person. Such changes are brought forth in writings, hymns, songs, prayers or reflected in our works. Thus, revealing the power of spiritual living to please God.

Do I dare to stand up and face other people with these words? Not for showmanship purposes, but simply, as the hymn says "Let it shine." Then give the Lord the credit for having had the opportunity. Christians have been doing this for centuries. It should be mentioned that the psalmist, David, admitted his weaknesses and Paul confessed his delinquencies before God. For God knows our nakedness. Anything I do in this book is not to be construed as trying to supersede God, the prophets, the disciples or the church of Christ. It is offered to bear witness to our struggles in life. I do not possess the mental or spiritual capacity to claim such a holy level of thinking as to comprehend God's Will. I am an ant on a mountain attempting to find a niche in God's Kingdom, especially here on earth. For I possess all the same weaknesses and faults of all people who walk the face of this planet. Yet, we are encouraged to report our spiritual growth that gives our purpose to serve Him.

Psalm 139: O Lord, You have searched me and know me.
You know my sitting down and my rising up:
You understand my thoughts afar off.
You comprehend my path and my lying down:
And are acquainted with my ways.
For there is not a word on my tongue,
Except "The Wonder of it all."
But behold, O Lord, You know it altogether.
You have hedged me behind and before,
And laid your hand upon me;
Such knowledge is too wonderful for me:
It is high, I can not attain it!
Psalm 105: Oh, give thanks to the Lord!
Call upon His name;
Make known His deeds among the peoples!
Sing to Him, sing psalms to Him;
Talk of His wondrous works!

Glory in His name;
Let the hearts of those rejoice who see the Lord!
Seek the Lord and His strength;
Seek His face forevermore!
Remember His marvelous works which He has done.

The theme of this book gives credit to God as a form of remembrance for the gifts God has granted to me (us). Most of these relates to God's Creative Genius, not excluding His saving grace. Many of these things are beyond description and comprehension. Therefore, it behooves us to bow our heads and simply say "Thank you, Lord!" "For the Lord is good, sing praises unto his name; for it is pleasant."(Psalm 135:3, KJ) This book is a portfolio of poems, songs, writings and visual imagery to assist in the awareness of God's benevolence. As Christians we all have a passion to be in partnership with our Heavenly Father, our heavenly Host, our Creator, our Redeemer and our eternal hope, there is a relevance to this pursuit. I am not an ordained minister, yet I am an integral part of God's affairs. I am the average Johnny Joe down the street attempting to follow Jesus with a growing faith, an image a far cry from His Holiness.

There is a reason and a purpose that forcefully primed my desire to step forward with the motivation to discover and capture in these essays the essence of our Lord's relentless calling. Such a calling by the spirit of Christ is evident and revealed in many ways. For God is a God of great variety. God's diversity of dealing with people to bring them to the base of the cross is beyond comprehension, yet we are all subject to it. The Bible confirms and validates that premise. This book is living proof of how one person not only approached God, but salvation as well. Searching, seeking, discovering, asking and reading became a pursuit to find the ingredients for spiritual fulfillment. As a result of this adventure, I now embrace the future with anticipation and optimism. The cross has been claimed and the spiritual compass points to Christ's promises that lie ahead. We are not alone "For Christ is with us!" This is what makes Christian life a progressive challenge. Not to respond to Christ's calling leaves us mired in self-indulgence and wasted faith, a life of depression without hope and purpose. For me this meant many years of coping with everyday mood swings and spiritual deprivation. To escape, I proceeded to explore "The Wonder of it all." There upon to embrace the liberty with an open mind to uncover the "Wonders" of what God has put on our plates. Don't ignore the calling. Each hymn that was written was a calling. Each Christian book written was a calling. Each Christian poem or stained glass piece of work is a calling. Each awakening morning and each sunset is a calling to use our gifts to praise the leader of humankind. It is faith in action that magnifies His faith, His love and His works in us. "Let your light shine before men, that they may see your good deeds and praise your Father in heaven." (Matt. 5:16, KJ) However, I shall temper that with Paul's words.. "Not that I have already obtained all this, or have already been made perfect, but I press on to take hold of that for which Christ Jesus took hold of me. Brothers, I do not consider myself yet to have taken hold of it. But one thing I do: forgetting what is behind and straining forward toward what is ahead, I press on toward that goal to win the prize for which God has called me heaven ward in Christ Jesus." (Phil. 3:12-14, IBML)

I must be honest with you, I am a neophyte when it comes to Biblical interpretation, for I am not a Biblical scholar. The content of this book serves a threefold purpose. One is to reveal the fruits of seeking God's attention. Secondly, to share the rewards of the labor of this compilation of thoughts. Thirdly, to please God, for we are His workmanship. The cover of this book carries this inscription, "Free as an eagle to praise the Lord."

Christianity is about sharing so that all of us can together grow in faith, in terms of this work some people may want to charge me with manipulating God. Some may even go to the extent of saying "You are doing this for money by selling a book." Not true! Some may say it is an intrusion into God's affairs. Rather than using the word intrusion, I prefer to use the word investigation, for that is precisely what our Lord wants us to do. He says " Seek and ye shall find." It is necessary to probe into God's magnificence in order to discover, learn, understand and accept things into our personal creed. It reinforces our faith. There are two poems included in these writings that address that issue, "Come and See" and "Awaken Thy Soul."

Perhaps a pertinent thought should be injected at this time. When approaching such a subject as this, justification and appropriateness of what is being said should be taken into consideration. Therefore, I resort to the voice of Jesus and a comment made by one of his disciples.

Jesus said, "Don't stop him, for he does it in my name." Inclusive also, "....keep this forever in the imagination of the thoughts of the heart...." (1 Chron. 29:18, KJ) "Having then gifts differing according to the grace that is given us, whether prophesy, let us prophesy according to the proportion of faith." (Rom 12:6, KJ) Sometimes imagination is critical to the interpretation of scripture. "There are diversities of gifts, but the same spirit." (1 Cor. 12:4, KJ) Note: If these gifts are not examined and practiced they will whither away. Perhaps this would be an appropriate time to state this saying "I am not perfect, just forgiven." This next scripture reading explains it better. "....behold, I say unto you lift up your eyes, and look on the fields; for they are white already to harvest. And he that reapeth receiveth wages, and gathered fruit unto life eternal: that both he that soweth and he that reapeth may rejoice together. And herein is that saying true, one soweth and another reapeth." (John 4:35, KJ) The Bible reminds us that there is a season for everything. Perhaps, this is my season to sow and others to reap. For Jesus said, "Reason together for the benefit of all", In the annals of history I make a small dent, but God recognizes and acknowledges each of our contributions. "But the manifestation of the Spirit is given to each one for the profit of all." (1 Cor. 12:7, KJ)

While worshiping the Lord in our works, it is not only the accomplishment, but the giving that is important. Each achievement serves as a stepping stone into the future. The reward is that it further inspires us to continue on with a more convincing faith. Also, it brings joy to the heart, for it proclaims God's goodness and the spirit to be productive in the spirit. These works are a speck in God's Master Plan, yet, they are important to the whole scheme of living. Just as each molecule is important to our body, each atom to the universe, each breath of air to living and each effort we make in the Body of Christ for our rebirth into His righteousness. "The Wonder of it all" is reflected in us all as a provision made by God to serve others. A provision by God to give testimony through our works. A provision to express gratitude through our works. A provision to discover in us the worthiness to proclaim God's grace through our grace, face to face and faith to faith standing in the presence and promises of Christ. And it shows forth in our beliefs and actions. "....that you may walk worthy of the Lord, fully pleasing him, being fruitful in every good work and increasing in the knowledge of God." (Col, 1:10, KJ) Yes, we all have gifts we can utilize in our works. Therefore, we should add to the list of wonders things God has accomplished in us, the "Wonders of His gifts in us."

Jesus said "Love each other." Love is expressed through a great variety of expressions. The fulfillment of this emotion can be writing letters, poems, books or singing a hymn to praise our Lord, thus revealing our most intiment thoughts. Let us not forget that love can be expressed through our hands. Such is the case with the stained glass work in photographs also shown in this book. Not only do they express love for Jesus Christ, our savior, but they also serve as a visual method to communicate a belief in Christianity.

Though I have a limited vision of God's domain and lack certified credentials, God still endows within me the spiritual desire to venture in the world of "The Wonder of it all", therein discovering new dimensions to our identity and our purpose for living. "For we are His workmanship, created in Christ Jesus for good works, which God prepared before hand that we should walk in them." (Eph. 2:10, KJ) God placed His signature on each soul for a special reason, ours to have and behold. Indeed, a very special gift. However, it is often taken for granted. As a person searches and explores, new dimensions come into view that modify, prepare and usher us into the future, many times derived from the past. Not to venture into the unknown perpetuates ignorance. The reward of the adventure is to acquire a better grasp of God's genius and living grace, despite the hazards of living on earth. In that pursuit, there is a realized trumph that reinforces our faith. From simple faith to one that possesses a wider spectrum of understanding, faith yields to grace. It is important to unshackle the mind and spirit and move toward knowing Christ and make him known.

This book is a compilation of thoughts that are the result of some things personal, some things borrowed, some things hand made and scriptural passages from God's Word. "And let us consider one another in order to stir up love and good works." (Heb. 10:24, KJ) If I could put the purpose for writing these words of thought in a nutshell,

I would indeed announce those words. The primary thrust of the book is to encourage the non-believers, especially the spiritually deprived, hoping to instill a sense that there is hope on the horizon. I believe that the book surrounds and envelops the theme "The Wonder of it All." My reward will be that in some small way it will inspire you as much as it has inspired me. Thanks for reading it. I remain your friend in Christ.

The Serenity Prayer

God grant me the serenity to accept the things I cannot change; the courage and the wisdom to know the difference. Living one day at a time; enjoying one moment at a time; Accepting hardship as the pathway to peace, taking as He did, this sinful world as it is, not as I would have it; trusting that he will make things right, if I surrender to His Will; That I may be reasonably happy in this life and supremely happy with Him, forever in the next. Amen

PERSONAL PRAYER

Our heavenly Father, our Heavenly Host, our Creator, our redeemer and our eternal hope that rests in your hands, these words I submit. I acknowledge and praise Your creative genius for it satisfies my hunger and my pleasures while I dwell on earth. I give thanks for the countless blessings you have bestowed on me and my family. It is in sincere gratitude that I recognize the free gift that you have granted me through the voluntary gracious act that your Son, Christ Jesus, performed on the cross. For it quickens my steps to march forward in my faith. Lord, please keep working on my soul and purpose in life as I with meager skills and knowledge proceed to write "The Wonder of it all". If I trespass into your domain, it is to discover, understand and accept more clearly your love, forgiveness and saving grace. May the eyes who read these words or the ears who hear them find a little hope to intertwine into their faith. From a person who is walking through life in the presence of our Lord.

RG

Psalm 37:3-5 Trust in the Lord, and do good;
Dwell in the land, and feed on His faithfulness.
Delight yourself also in the Lord,
And He shall give you the desires of your heart.
Commit your way to the Lord.

Psalm 111 "He has made His wonderful works to be remembered;

WITH GOD'S PERMISSION

The silent mind is wastefull to the soul and to other people. Hymn: "Lift Your Hearts, Raise Your Voice." Ecc. 5:3 IBML "A dream comes through much activity." This book is my dream come true where the activity of my heart, hands ands spirit has guided me along an adventurous journey that made it possible. It set the stage for writing the manuscript for this book. What a high honor and privelege it is when He entrusts us with His image, His Spirit, His works, His proclamations and His blessings to be a disciple of God. As His son's and daughter's we are on assignment to know Him and to make Him known.

Before under taking the assignment of writing a Christian book we must take into consideration the prerequisite for justification. Who grants us that option in our life? We need to examine ourselves to determine our worthiness and whether or not we have pretentous reasons. Our integrity is at stake. We have to answwer the question "Is it done with an open mind in the right spirit?" Does our vision have the right Christian perspective" The following scripture readings lay the ground work and serve as a foundation to work from. If we use the right guide lines, then we should not be ashamed to do work in the name of Jesus Christ.

2 Cor. 5:20 IBML "Now then, we are ambassadors of Christ, as thought God were appealing through us, we employ you on Christ's behalf, be reconciled to God." Forwe are His messengers.

Heb. 13:5 KJ "....the fruit of our lips giving thanks to his name."

Col. 2:2 KJ "....to ask that you may be filled with knowledge of His will in all wisdom and spiritual understanding, that you may work worthy of the Lord, fully pleasing Him. being fruitful in every good work."

Psalm 11:9 KJ "Blessed are they that keep his testimony and seek him with the whole heart." We are his seeker, but it must be done for genuine reasons.

Rom. 3:34 KJ "Being justified freely by His grace through redemption that is in Jesus Christ." If we proceed in accordance to the free spirit of Christ we have that liberty.

Deu. 4:29 KJ "You shall find the Lord, your God, if you seek with all your heart and soul." That was the resultant of "The Wonder Of It All."

Prov. 3:5 IBML "In all your ways acknowledge Him, and He will direct your path."

2 Cor. 8:11 KJ "....but now you must also complete the doing of it; that as there was readiness to desire it, so then also may it be a completion of what you." By the grace of God's Will we all have that entitlement.

2 Cor. 9:8 KJ "In doing so, He wants us to be filled with the spirit in our doings and our goings." No matter where we go in our goings.

Heb. 6:11 IBML "....show the same diligence to the full assurance.... that you do not become sluggish." We must engage for the sake of Chrisitanity.

1 Tim. 4:14 KJ "Neglect not the gift that is in thee."

Rom. 12:6 KJ "Having gifts that differ according to the grace given us, let us use them."

Eph. 4:1 KJ "Walk worthy of the vocation where with you are called." Writing this book and ministering with stained glass is works (vocation) in God's eyes.

2 Cor. 10:17 KJ "But he who glories. let him glory in the Lord." Hopefully, my works help to draw attention to His name as well as magnifies His image.

Heb. 13:5 KJ "By Him, therefore, let us offer the sacrifice of our praise to God continually, that is, the fruits of our lips giving thanks to His name. But to do good and to communicate forget not; for with such sacrifice God is well pleased."

When we write a book, poem or a hymn we are are sacrificing our time and praise.

1 Cor. 12:7 IBML "But one and the same spirit works all these things, distributing to each individually as He wills." God's will influences our will.

2 Cor. 9:8 KJ "So let each one give as he purposes in his heart." Via my writings and works I have revealed what is in my heart.

Psalm 4:13 KJ "Trust in the Lord, and be good.... and he shall give us the desires of our hearts."

Phil. 4:13 KJ "I can do all things through Christ will strengthened me." In life as we progress through "The Wonder Of It All" our spirit will be made stronger and as the result be fortified.

Rom. 15:13 KJ ".....that ye may abound in hope, through the power of the Holy Spirit." It is the spirit that provides the courage to face challenges as well as do good deeds.

Matt. 5:16 KJ "Let your light so shine before men, that they may see yourgood works and glorify your Father which is in heaven."

Titus 3:8 KJ "This is a faithful saying and these things I will that thou affirm constantly that they which believe in God might be carefull to maintain good works. These things are good and profitable unto man.." May my works be profitable in your life.

Phil. 4:18 KJ "Finally, brethren, whatever things are true, whatever things are noble, whatever things are just, if there is any virtue and if there is anything praiseworthy, meditate on these things." If we meditate on "The Wonder Of It All" wonderful insights will develope.

1 Cor. 15:58 KJ "Be steadfast immoveable, always abounding in the works of the Lord, knowing that in the Lord your work is not in vain." He is giving us assurance, if we do things in his name.

Eph. 2:10 KJ "For we are His workmanship created in Christ Jesus unto good works."

Matt. 12:35 KJ "A good man out of the good treasures of his heart bringeth forth good things."

Exk. 36:26 IBML :And I will give you a new heart and put a new spirit in you."

Mark 9:39 KJ "Jesus said "Don't stop him, because anyone who uses my name to do powerful things will not easily say evil things about me."

Mark 7:17 KJ "But also look at the faith, in whose name is the work done?" Therefore, we are given the freedom and liberty to write about the glory of God.

Rom. 10:13 KJ "Whoever believes in him will not be put to shame.

James 2:24 KJ "Ye see them how by works man is justified, and not be faith only." There is more to Christianity than faith.

James 2:26 KJ "For as the body without the spirit is dead, so faith without works is dead also." In our deeds our faith and grace should instill in us a sense of doing good works through the image and spirit of Christ.

John 3:18 KJ "My children let us not love in words or in tongue, but in deeds and truth."

Heb. 10:24 KJ " Let us consider one another to stir up love and good works."

Rom. 15:2 KJ "Let everyone of us please his neighbor for his edification." By way of "The Great Commission" that is our God given assignment and responsibility.

Phil. 1:16 KJ "Be confident of this very thing, that God has begun a good work in you and will complete it...."

Ezk 36:256 IBML "And I (Jesus) will give you a new heart and put a new spirit within you." This book "The Wonder Of It All" has put a new spirit and life in me.

Matt. 16:27 KJ "For the Son of man shall come in the glory of his Father, His angels and then he shall reward every man (all Christian's) to his works." The ultimate reward is everlasting life.

THE WONDER OF IT ALL

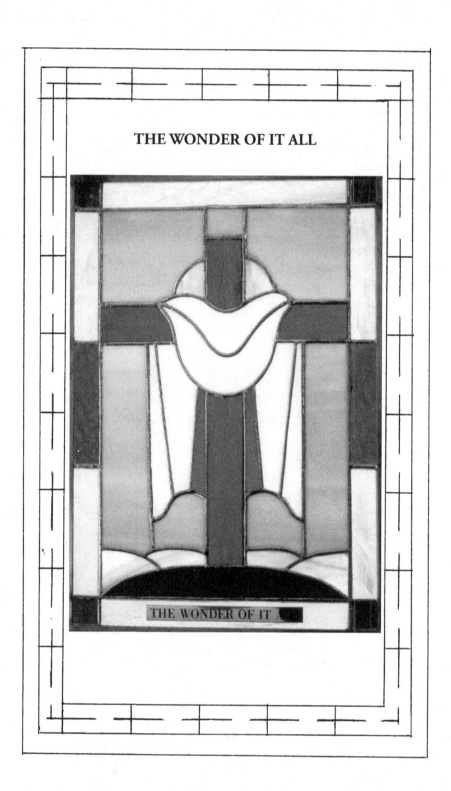

THE WONDER OF IT A

CHAPTER 1:

INTRODUCTION

As we look through the window of "The Wonder of it all" we discover many things about God's creative genius, His love and mercy through the grace of His redemptive powers. Our intuition should make us aware of the fact that there exists an author greater than us and that a spirit emanates from that source influencing our daily lives. The mind is made for exploration as evidenced by a look at history, educational systems and the development of people with ideas revealing their genius. The human mind has and always will have the desire to probe into God's Creation and the workings of the Holy Spirit. Out of such exploration emerges greater insight to "The Wonder of it all." One must engage in order to encounter that which surrounds us as well as that which is invisible, seeking, searching, probing or exploring the vastness of God's Domain. Out of this is a path leading to trust and faith in God's forecast for a promised land. God gave us our mind, body, heart and soul to be programmed as an investment to reveal and spread God's message. Scripture: John 4:48 "Jesus said, "Unless you see signs and wonders you will in no way believe". Christ is the body of the church, however, without us the church could not function. That challenge and responsibility has been assigned to Christians to magnify and glorify His sovereignty. Through us the church is active in the world. It is our responsibility to open "The Book of Life." Such inquires require a quiet place, patience, and the ability to focus and concentrate on God's gifts. Even prayer enters the picture, opening the heart and mind to embrace the "Wonders of it all." Rather than let dictums govern our thinking, incorporate the practice of imagination. Imagination brings into play and view a more realistic interpretation of God's creative genius and His redemptive grace, thereby serving as cohesive elements to bind the various aspects of faith together. It solidifies and weaves the fabric of faith as a pathway to follow and cross the bridge into the out stretched arms of our Lord. It is a walk through reality, yet, it guides us like a compass as we travel through our episodes of life on earth.

We were made in the image of God. To infuse that into our daily living, not only requires exploration, but imagination as well. Self image as well as robbing ourselves in an image to please our maker. He gave birth to our image. Reflection on how we become that image and how that image transforms us takes shape over time. Jesus made us aware that our thinking processes are integral to establishing a positive relationship with the Father of our being. The 1st commandment gives us a clue to one of the most important ingredients to satisfy God's expectations needed in our devotional life. The commandments tell us to love thy God and love thy neighbor as they self. This sets the stage and essentially says " If you love me, receive my grace and tell your neighbors." To become a genuine Christian, requires a transformation of values and attitude, including modification of ones self image. A mind that is willing to be molded to become Christ like. The key is willingness, taking the initiative to open the mind, heart, and soul to allow the Holy Spirit to dwell in us permitting God to perform His work. It is not an immediate injection of mature faith, for like any discipline it is acquired in stages. God knows that and sympathizes with our struggles. An Olympic runner doesn't run a world record the first time he steps on the track to compete. A teacher, lawyer, or doctor doesn't become a certified professional until his mind has been trained to perform his specialty. In God's eyes, Christians are His elect, however, there is a preparedness necessary to take on the assignment of Christianity. It is the infusion of a spirit outside ourselves that transforms us so that we may think and conduct ourselves like Christ. Such characterization and actions are revealed through our thoughts and actions on a daily basis. Ideas that are grounded in what God offers us through His word, discovery of gifts granted through His creative genius and the realization (revelation) of redemption through the spiritual power of His Son, Jesus Christ. Therefore, do not be afraid to engage the freedom of imagination as it applies to God's wonders, for it holds promises for all the tomorrows. Until a person becomes aware of God and His providence for each of us, our soul will decay and wither into a useless body not worthy of God's attention. Bones will simply dry white, rather than a creation wrapped in worthiness to be granted that which Jesus proclaimed as our birth right and be crowned with his glory for eternity. The final episode of "The Wonder of it All". It is to reap the harvest of God's grace, love, mercy and freedom to live eternally in peace. Wow! To live forever in the Kingdom of God. What a grand vision full of great expectations. Hopefully, this will help you to scan the panoramic view of God's works.

Each person has the same unadulterated right to accomplish what has been presented in this re'sume' of thoughts. Let your mind explore God's gifts. Lay captive each clue God whispers through "The Wonder of it All" for it will eventually yield the true nature of God. Lay claim to what is your birthright. As evidenced in this collection of thoughts there are several ways by which we can explore the mastery of God's ways. Don't be afraid to set pen to paper letting God know your most intimate thoughts. Whether it be scribed in words, composed in a song, the rhythm of a poem, or letting the hands speak by fabricating stained glass images to reveal visionary ideas, God will listen, he will acknowledge and appreciate knowing you as an individual. He will not cast you out, nor should any faithful Christian brother/sister. The more we explore, the more we'll discover ourselves as well as Jesus Christ.

There is a reason for the resurrection of our Lord. It is free, claim it. Otherwise God would be dishonored. All that work by His creative genius, the grace of salvation and we don't take notice. God would respond by saying "Shame on you". He who hesitates shall miss the boat traveling to a destination. The challenge is knowing how to tap into the source of it all, it is a power that emanates from only one true God. He controls the throttle and we become the benefactors, in that our gratitude should well up from our souls. Our mouths and hearts should shout the words "Thank You, Lord" for "The Wonder of it All." "....but be ye transformed by the renewing of your mind, that ye may prove what is the good and acceptable and perfect will of God." (Rom. 12:2,KJ) "The man who plants and the man who waters have one purpose, and each will be rewarded according to his own labor, for we are God's fellow workers. You are God's field and God's building."(I Cor. 3:8,KJ)

HYMN: "THE WONDER OF IT ALL"

There's the wonder of sunset at evening.
The wonder as sunrise I see.
But the wonder of wonders that thrills my soul,
Is the wonder that God loves me.

There's the wonder of spring-time and harvest.
The sky, the stars, the sun.
But the wonder of wonders that thrills my soul,
Is a wonder that's only begun.

O the wonder of it all, the wonder of it all.
Just to think that God loves me.
O the wonder of it all, the wonder of it all.
Just to think that God loves me.

George Beverly Shea
C 1957 Word Music, LLC

I BELIEVE

I believe for every drop of rain that falls, a flower grows,
I believe that somewhere in the darkest night, a candle glows.
I believe for everyone who goes astray, someone will come to show the way.
I believe, I believe.

I believe above a storm the smallest prayer can still be heard.
I believe that someone in the great somewhere hears every word.

Every time I hear a new born baby cry.
Or touch a leaf or see the sky.
Then I know why, I believe.

CROSSING LIFE'S BRIDGES

Through life we walk,
crossing many bridges.
Of this journey, I now talk,
The genetic code of life,
passed through the ages.
Then we turn the pages,
now let us recall the stages.

First we are born,
then through infancy we struggle.
Without parents we would be forlorn,
they bestow their love with a cuddle.
Then we encounter youth and the teenage years,
many time experiencing fears.
Our parents' love dried the tears,
helping us to the future peer.

Then on to adulthood,
with the responsibilities of manhood.
And woman with motherhood,
with Christ teaching us to live in brotherhood.
The final bridge to cross is from life to the eternal realm,
with Christ Jesus at the helm.
But wait, there is another bridge to cross,
before we reach the cross.

We must cross the bridge of salvation,
there is no other conclusion.
For it is our transgressions,
when forgiven by Christ it gives new direction.
Salvation is a special bridge to cross,
Christ gave it to us on the cross.
Redemption for our soul to cleanse,
like the purity of a crystal lens.

Birth....to youth....to adulthood we all must pass.
Salvation...to Christian brotherhood...to Christ's care we pass.
before we can reach the cross, without alas !
Christ helps us to cross the bridge to God's eternal plan each
day.
May God bestow His blessings on us each day.
The bridges of our life,
rest in God's Grace !
Through Him we are given new life,
then God we can embrace.   RG

GIVE WHAT YOU CAN

It may be just a trifling bit,
that you may have to give,
But give it, for to someone else,
it may mean hope to live!

Give what you can, although it may,
seem too small to bestow.
A gift is measured by its size,
how well the needy know !

A wise man said, "The only wealth
we have is what we share."
Then give. Who knows, your gift may be,
an answer to a prayer !

Esther Nilssom

MAY IT HELP

I discovered things along the way,
hopefully, they'll help you on this day.
For life is worthwhile living,
let your faith provide the giving.
Don't let life get you down,
spirit up, please don't drown.
Though I am only human,
festering with flaws.
These thoughts within me remain,
and there is purpose to my cause.
As God is my witness,
it may not be my best.
To some it may be nonsense,
although it helped me to face the test.

A story told in God's presence,
now you know the rest.

RG

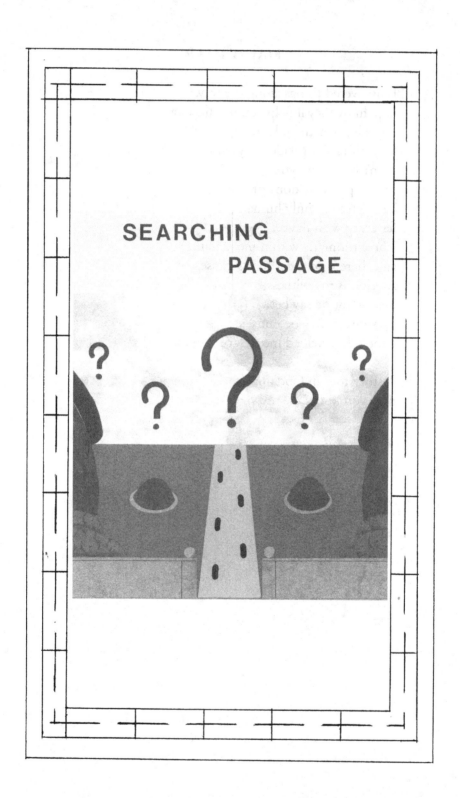

CHAPTER 2:

SEARCHING PASSAGE

Birth to death we all make the passage,
searching for God's message.
A life is written like a book, page by page,
day to day searching, searching, forever searching.

The Good Book tells of heaven's host,
God's spirit dwelling as a ghost.
God, why do you hide? Never seen, felt or heard.
Yet intertwined like a thread.
Your spirit calling, calling, forever calling.

In my soul your spirit please reside,
God, how do I confide?
Expose yourself, harbor in me,
Your presence so that I see.
Your presence I could believe,
my soul surely would relieve.
A soul yearning, yearning, forever yearning.

God please guide my passage,
endow me with the courage.
Life's journey seeking the bondage,
a soul seeking, seeking, forever seeking.

To the cross I am reaching,
Christ's love and his teaching.
Through him my redemption,
His promise is my salvation.
There stands the revelation,

to the cross, reaching, reaching,
                    forever reaching.
My soul forever searching.
My soul forever calling.
My soul forever yearning.
My soul forever seeking.
My soul forever reaching.

When shall I hear your voice?
to fill the soul with elated rejoice.
My soul traveling through life's passage,
a soul wanting with endless courage.
This I have endured from childhood to old age.
With faith in the Good Book message,
learning while on life's stage.   RG

THE SEEKER

"....thou shalt seek the Lord they God, thou shalt find him,
If thou seek him with all thy heart and with all the soul."
(Deu. 4:29, KJ)

God, I am your seeker.
How do I find you with spirit growing weaker?

Looking and wanting for so may years,
hoping and praying to calm the fears.

They tell of Your glory,
disciples reveal their story.

Plant in my soul the spiritual flower,
let it blossom each living hour.

From doubt's bondage I must flee,
grant me the blessing to be set free.

I beseech you, let me find the treasure,
so that I can journey in blissful pleasure.

Let it be a joy to stay,
instilling a glad heart, come what may.

RG

"....that he is a rewarder of them that diligently seek him."
(Heb. 11:6, KJ)

IS GOD A DELUSION ?

Is God a delusion?
Some form that conclusion.
Wrong is such an affliction.
They ignore God's creation.

God's truth that disciples gave translation;
His word has the information.
God's gifts showing affection,
His deeds are the inspiration.

Now it's time to give explanation,
though not done in transgression.
But said to give vision.
Now listen to this version,
spirit to soul in transition.

Below are His blessings given full count,
Each day, awe the amount.
Acknowledge and give account.
Praise, joy, hope singing out.

Our body now to ponder;
surely a great wonder.
Eyes for seeing all the beauty.
Ears for hearing sounds aplenty.
Voice for singing unto thee.
Sense of feeling; danger, sadness, joy, love, injury.
Heart beating with energy.
Lungs breathing airs vitality.
Mind for thinking: mathematics, music, writing, ingenuity.
All together forming our body. All working in unity.
Yes, this is man/woman. What creativity!

So ask yourself with all sincerity,
is God to man a delusion ?
Look around at all creation,
how can you form any other conclusion ?
No, God is not a delusion.
this should be our observation.
A soul filled with elation,
should be our reaction.

RG

HOW DO I KNOW THERE IS A GOD ?

I know each time I look at my wife.
I know when a new child is born.
I know each time I see my children, grandchildren and friends.
I know each time I receive and give love.
I know each time the sun rises.
I know because of life in its various forms.
I know when beautiful flowers grow and bloom.
I know each time I catch a fish on the line.
I know when it rains and the streams flow.
I know because God gave us the capacity to think, design and develop new technologies.
I know because God gave us the raw material resources to survive on earth.
I know each time a bird flies or a deer runs.
I know because of God's artistic gallery on display.
I know because the Bible tells me so.
I know because of God's love, mercy and grace.
I know because God accepts me as I am.
I know because of the Holy Spirit that guides me.
I know because of God's only begotten Son, Jesus Christ.
I know because I believe and trust.

RG

TAKEN FOR GRANTED

Taking for granted the days of our lives,
one day at a time God gives.
Seldom thoughts about from where we came,
God thinks, "What a sinful shame."

Onward we march seeking personal goals,
as life rapidly unfolds.
Day to day writing our life's story,
controlling forces which our soul destroy.

From childhood to adulthood,
demands we withstood,
Education or skills to learn,
working for money to earn.
Families to raise and bills to pay,
responsibilities every day.

Other interests attract our attention,
so many there are to mention.
Living in a world of varied issues,
Oh, the confusion that ensues.

Social and political problems world wide,
all impedes our stride.
Forces which become all consuming,
there tasks we are assuming.

The spirit of our soul becomes lost,
what a dreadful cost.
Perhaps God looks down in confusion,
knowing our need for His intercession.

Taking for granted the days of our lives,
one day at a time God gives.
Each dawning should have His guidance,
each glowing with radiance.

Each day we take for granted,
none can be recanted.
Cherish those He has granted,
respond by not taking God for granted.

RG

THE MYSTRERIOUS SPELL

What is the spell that controls the universe?
What is the spell that tells the seeds to sprout?
What is the spell that causes the plants to grow and buds that burst into flowers?
What is the spell that fills the air with scented fragrance?
What is the spell that compels the leaves on the plants and trees to reach the sky?
What is the spell that lures the mother bird to it fledgling's nest?
What is the spell that compels all things to grow?
What is the spell that bonds man and women in marriage?
What is the spell that gives life to a new-born infant?
What is the spell that says all things must die ?
What is the spell that bonds humankind in the grasp of universal love ?
What is this mysterious spell over which God presides ?
Where is the spell in our hearts to "Give Thanks" for the wonderful spell ?

What a marvelous spell!!

RG

CHAPTER 3:

GOD. THE INVISIBLE ONE

Job. 11:7" Canst thou by searching find out God?"

God, our Father in heaven. We pray to Him and put our trust in Him. Yet, we don't see him face to face. We can't touch Him to shake hands and say good morning or say "Thank you!" for your many blessings. Thank you for your creative genius and your saving grace. Thank you for life. The Bible tells us that He loves us dearly as one of His children. He can't physically hug us with a loving embrace. He can't pat us on the back and say "Well done faithful servant." Because of God's invisibility we many times utter the words "God, where are you?" Thus, feeling the rejection or lack of the presence of God in our lives, even to the point of sensing that we have been forsaken. So the question arises :What is God like?" The Bible tells us that he has an image. However, we can't sculpture a physical image of what God looks like. Therefore, he takes on the image of a ghost. How do we communicate with a ghost?

To answer these questions we must turn to the only source available to us. Of course, that is the word of God. By examining some key scripture readings we should be able to form some resemblance of our maker. The Commander in chief of the human race and our world. None of us have ever seen God. Therefore, we can only rely on what people have told us down through the ages. Christianity is about sharing our knowledge of His creative and forgiving powers. Knowledge leads to understanding and truth. The truth being something we can put faith and trust in. If God governs our affairs and our destination, then we should know "What he is like."

Because of the magnitude of God's authority and power in comparison to our limited comprehensive abilities, our smallness as a person creates a problem. How do we measure up to the greatness of His Holy image? Yet, the Bible tells us that we are made in His image. This clearly depicts our restrictions to model his character. We are not capable of harboring such a perfect image. Therefore, we are faced with the challenge of trying to the best of our ability to satisfy God's expectations of us and infuse the standards set forth in the likeness of Christ. By choice it is a God given assignment in life. We have to remember that Christ was God in the human flesh, sent to us to portray the image of God. It is through Jesus that we learn that God has personality and character. His traits would be an individual study in itself. In addition, we discover in the Old Testament the power of God's sovereignty over humanity. These things must be studied to determine "What God is like?

Now to be more specific, let us turn to some scripture readings from the Bible. Actually Jesus tells us a very few words. Jesus said "God is Spirit." "God is Spirit: and they that worship him must worship him in "Spirit" and truth." (John 4:24, KJ) So when we pray Father, Son and Holy Ghost, the ghost is spirit. After Christ was resurrected and was raised from the dead he left behind a spirit by which he could relate to us and we could communicate with him through the spirit. For us it is a sense of an indwelling spirit that gives us direction in life as well as a feeling of well being spiritually. It is like love, it just exists. "And when Jesus had cried with a loud voice, he said, Father, into thy hands I commend my spirit; and having said thus, he gave us the ghost, in doing so he give up the ghost (spirit) to us. We have and behold it through his grace. (Luke 23:46,KJ) Luke 24:39 gives us further insight to the origin of the spirit. "Behold my hands and my feet, that it is I myself, handle me, and see; for a spirit hath not flesh and bones, as ye see me have."

When we submit our selves to Jesus for salvation, it a spiritual encounter. By way of the spirit we receive a reward by his grace and power of redemption, "....so everyone that is born of the Spirit." (John 3:8,KJ) The Bible tells us that we must be born again to enter into the heavenly realm of God's kingdom. It is a renewing of a person spiritually. We are changed into a new creature. This instills a sense to be in harmony with God and change our ways. It fosters a need to modify our thinking processes as well as our conduct. If the commitment to Jesus is genuine we are compelled to be in tune with the likeness of him. Thus producing a different orientation to God and to life. We become a model showing forth the internalization of the power of the spirit of Christ. Actually, the presence of him is found every where around the world all at the same time. It is a spirit that encapsulates the entire universe. It is with us every day of the year. It doesn't matter where we are; in church, eating breakfast or driving a car. It is like the blood of our body, Christ's blood (Spirit) is always with us until the end of the age. He can be called upon anywhere or any time. "He that hath ear, let him hear what the Spirit saith unto the churches."(Rev.2:7,KJ) Whether it be in a Sunday morning service or a special celebration, we petition for His presence. "For through Him we both have access to the Father in one spirit." (Eph. 2:18,KJ) "And he who searches our hearts knows the mind of the Spirit." (Rom. 8:26,KJ) Yes, God is a Spirit! "The Wonder of His Spirit."

RG

A self-image in the Image of God

God created man, male and female, in his own image. What an awesome reality that is. Here I am in the first chapter of the Bible, a woman, distinguished from animals, distinguished from my male counterpart, and literally created in the image of God. Certainly womanhood was no afterthought with God, and it was through the creation of both male and female that God has offered his fullest self-revelation.

If somehow in our imagination we are able to recreate all the qualities of perfect man and perfect woman in one being, we have, perhaps, a faint hint of who God really is. And, as we reflect on who God is, we see a picture of the image we carry in ourselves individually. Unfortunately, that image of God often bears virtually no resemblance to our own image. The reason for that according to many Christian counselors, is because many of us suffer from a low self-image. But how can our self-image be low when we contemplate the image of God in which we were created? Personally, I find that my self-esteem is lowest when I am least reflecting the image of God. Indeed, my self-esteem has very little to do with the ego-boosting gratification that comes with awards, promotions, bonuses, and new clothes. These are the temporary "uppers" of the "me-generation", but they are not what builds a healthy self-image.

I feel best about myself, not when I read a flattering review of one of my books or when I am wearing a new outfit, but when I have selflessly reached out to someone in need and given with no thought of reward or of self. It is only when my self is submerged that God's image begins to shine forth. Then I have a healthy self-image that truly reflects God's image.

Author: Ruth A Tucker

IN HIS IMAGE

"So God created man in is own image." (Gen. 1:27,KJ)

How do we come to interpreting and understanding this piece of scripture ? First and foremost God is invisible. He is the divine master of the universe and owner of the entire human race, to which is forever His glory. The Bible gives us the characteristics of God, but for the most part for the non-believer or Christian neophytes these escape our comprehension, both physically and spiritually. Not one single person out of the entire historical chain of humanity has ever seen God, except Christ. None of the prophets or disciples saw God the Father. Or, are we saying that God was in human flesh via the image of Christ ? If that were true, then we would have both a physical and spiritual description of God. However, Christ was in human flesh just like us. Is what Genesis tells us about our being in the image of God, a foretelling of Christ? Christ was not yet revealed at this early stage of the Bible. Image, what image ? Every human being born has a different physical appearance, therefore, none of us can look like God. Perhaps a figment of our imagination would suffice, where each of us clothes God to form our image of Him. Therefore, we can not sculpture God.

The Trinity: Father, Son and Holy Ghost. How do we deal with a "ghost?" We can not be the Father, the Son or the spirit of His imminence. That would place us on the same level as Him. That we know is an impossibility. We are not worthy. We can live in the spirit, but never as a perfect imitation of God. For we humans beings have limitations. God's authority and power separates us from Him. We are totally reliant on Him, not ourselves. The Bible tells us that if we were to look on God we would be blinded. Again, therefore, we can not recognize His image. Yes, He is a loving and forgiving God, but those are His personal attributes, not His physical image. The image that dwells in the heart and soul of a Christian, is a coexistence in spirit. Much like the air we breath in and out to sustain life. That is where the Holy Ghost comes into the Trinity. It is a spiritual vision.

Christ tells us that we will not see his Father until we pass through by His authority. He controls the gates. He is the gatekeeper. Therefore, we will not see the image of God until we leave this world, where death puts us on the path to the door to our heavenly home. Thanks be to Jesus Christ. It is fundamental to our Christian belief, our spiritual well -being, the church of Christ, and our image of God as well as our image in the eyes of God. Some say there must be more to "We are made in the image of God." The answer lays in Jesus Christ. If we take on the likeness of Jesus then we are dressed in the image of God.

The author of Gen. 1:27 did not give any specific answers to how we are created in God's image. Thus leaving in the minds of a reader an open ended question that initiates imagination, guessing and speculation based on individual knowledge or experience rather than concrete evidence. How can we be created in the image of God when we fall so very short of that image? It further perpetuates the problem of identifying and defining our image and shape according to God's expectations. Worship or freedom is not the answer, for they are our responsibility as Christians. I shall assume that many people who sit in the pew of our churches could not give an intelligent answer to "How are we made in the image of God." How do we dress ourselves in the image of God when He is the almighty and Holy Creator ? We do not, nor can we possess such powers. Therefore, there is a need for a more definitive interpretation. For it would form the spring board from which people can understand their identity and purpose of living in the image of Jesus, the invisible one.

THE INQUIRY

Paul tells us in describing the preeminence of Christ that "He, Christ, is the invisible God, the first born over all creation." (Col. 1:15,KJ) "He also predestined to be conformed to the image of His Son, that he might be the first born among many brethren. He is the image of the visible God, the first born over all creation." Romans 8:29 " Romans 8:24,25 "For we are saved by hope: but hope that is seen is not hope; for what a man seeth, why doth ye yet hope for." (Rom. 8:24,

KJ) but if we hope for what we do not see, then we eagerly wait for it with perseverance.... But the Spirit Himself makes intercession for us with groaning, which can not be uttered." Essentially this is telling us that this is an invisible affair coexisting in the spirit. Perhaps this could be referred as the "Great Expectation" where we are conjoined at the heart in the image of God. 2 Cor. 4:4 "In whom the God of this world hath blinded the minds of them which believe not, lest the light of the glorious gospel of Christ, who is the image of God." (2 Cor, 4:4, KJ) This speaks to the preparation of the mind through the workings of the Holy Spirit as alluded to in "Approaching Salvation." "And have put on the new man, which is renewed in knowledge after the image of him that created him." (Col.3:10, KJ) 1 Cor. 15:49 " "And as we have borne the image of the earthly, we shall also shall bear the image of the heavenly." (1 Cor. 15:49,IBML) All part of "The Wonder of it all."

"SO GOD CREATED MAN IN HIS OWN IMAGE"
(Gen. 1:27,KJ)

IMAGE OF GOD	IMAGE OF USE
God is Spirit	His spirit indwells us
God is God	We are not God
Invisible: No face to identity	We have a face
No audible voice	We have a voice
Can not touch Him	We can be touched
God's Will	We have a will
The creator of all things	Designer of earthly survival
The Master of the universe	We are the beneficary
God of wonders	We can't produce His wonders
The sovereign God	Impossible for us
The Holy One most high	Impossible for us
The Almighty One	Impossible for us
The heavenly Father	Impossible for us
The Holy Spirit	The spirit dwells in us
God of grace	We learn grace
God of mercy	We learn mercy
The righteous God	We learn rightousness
The just God: Judgment	We learn to judge fairly
The loving God: Caring	We learn to care
The immutable God: Never changing	We are unpredictable
God of veracity: Truth	We learn truth, how to identify it
Omnipresent: Everywhere	We are a community of people
Omnipotent: All powerful	Limited power
Omniscience: All knowing	Limited knowledge
Our Lord, Christ Jesus, the Son of God	He controls our destination
The Redeemer: Forgiveness of sins	We are imperfect
Keeper of the gate	Through Christ we see God
Issues eternal life: Promised through faith	We develop faith
Our advocate	He presents us to God
Our Lord, the King	Our spiritual leader
Our resurrection: Christ was risen	We can't save ourselves
Miracle worker	Christ demonstrates his power
Prince of life	Author of everlasting life
Prince of peace	Abiding in Him we find peace
Magnanimous	All loveing and forgiving

GOD'S PRESENCE

How do we know God's presence?
When we pray in deep reverence.

A spirit which should not lay dormant,
to us it is life's endowment.

Without it we have God's estrangement,
a soul lacking fulfillment.

God within grants us freedom,
a blessing from His Kingdom.
Now give us that wisdom.

God's presence giveth serenity,
a new life with quality.
This sense of Christianity.

Spirit and soul in unity,
acknowledge His majesty.
Of this there is certainty.

He leadeth with the trinity,
to show His sincerity.
A new life in eternity.

His love shows forth His great generosity,
instilling deep tranquility.
Dismissing anxiety.

A heart filled with bounty,
praises extended to thee.
Now peace and joy present be,
preserved for eternity.

RG

HOW DO I KNOW THERE IS A GOD ?

I know each time I look at my wife.
I know when a new child is born.
I know each time I see my children, grandchildren and friends.
I know each time I receive and give love.
I know each time the sun rises.
I know because of life in its various forms.
I know when beautiful flowers grow and bloom.
I know each time I catch a fish on the line.
I know when it rains and the streams flow.
I know because God gave us the capacity to think, design and develop new technologies.
I know because God gave us the raw material resources to survive on earth.
I know each time a bird flies or a deer runs.
I know because of God's artistic gallery on display.
I know because the Bible tells me so.
I know because of God's love, mercy and grace.
I know because God accepts me as I am.
I know because of the Holy Spirit that guides me.
I know because of God's only begotten Son, Jesus Christ.
I know because I believe and trust.

RG

DOES GOD REALLY CARE ?

The Bible tells of the good shepherd,
and that we are His flock.

For all humanity is a herd,
I will find you despite the size of the flock.

He knows our name and our pain,
when we have reason to complain.

He knows our face,
our identity, He can trace.

He knows every born child,
on that thought dwell awhile.

I have written your name,
and will be with you in your land.

When to me you call,
I'll find you on the roll call.

Express your needs to me,
for I'll be with thee.

In me place your trust,
as through life you thrust.

In the mean- time you must smile,
for I'll be along in a little while.

RG

LIFE: GOD'S PRESENT

God put life in our hands to hold,
treasure it for it is more precious than gold.

A special gift for us to claim,
so personal that we have a name.

With a soul that is free,
whatever life's blessings may be.

A soul that confronts each day,
as we journey along life's pathway.

Each morning anew we greet,
God's presence we must meet.

Face each day with a smile,
it makes it more worthwhile.

A heart that knows as time goes by,
that there is a purpose and a reason why.

The spirit to some will come,
but to others eternal mum.

A hand reaches down from above,
it is God showing His love.

Accept it with a smile,
let Him dwell for a while.

Be grateful as God's blessings you embrace,
given by His good grace.

This road that you trod,
prepared for you by God.

In your soul dismiss hatred and greed,
be a Christian and follow God's creed.

Then at life's journey end,
on God you can depend.

RG

LIFE FORCES

What is life, we ask ?
With mind to task,
to discover things so vast.
Present today and past.

Spring-time through summer,
seeds sprout reaching for the sky.
What's this force to which they reply?

In spring time trees bud,
leaves appear like extended hands.
Hands gather sun, on which it lands,
their appearance before planned.

Birds on wings fly,
gliding through the sky.
Their flight majestic certainty;
What is this force giving energy ?

All creatures earthly presence,
breathing on air for existence.
Breathing in life's force;
Oh, where is the source ?

Insects hatch and multiply,
quickly they scurry around.
Butterflies, how pretty they fly;
"Hurray! Life!" they shout.

Man a loving creature;
Love is a special feature.
He giveth in gesture.
He giveth in compassion.
He giveth in emotion.
A life force internal dwelling.

Love to express our caring.
Its origin, perhaps you're thinking ?

To survive nourishment we need,
food around us abounds.
God provides with special seed,
life everywhere surrounds.

One final need remains,
Spiritual life for us to sustain,
the reason is so plain.
God's spirit is our faith inside,
in our soul to reside.
God given for earthly life.
God given for spiritual life.

God given for eternal life.
Don't walk in peril or live in strife,
with forces present in earthly life.
Christ gave his life so that we would have everlasting life.

Life is a special blessing,
given for the asking.
Ever present day-to-day,
a gift sent our way.
Life is a miraculous force.
From where is the source ?
Should you ask? God of course !

Surely these life forces,
must be greater than cosmic forces,

RG

CROSSING LIFE'S BRIDGES

Through life we walk, crossing many bridges.
Of this journey, I now talk.

The genetic code of life,
passed through the ages.
Then we turn the pages,
now let us recall the stages.

First we are born,
then through infancy we struggle.
Without parents we would be forlorn,
they bestow their love with a cuddle.

Then we encounter youth and the teenage years,
many time experiencing fears.
Our parents' love dried the tears,
helping us to the future peer.

Then on to adulthood,
with the responsibilities of manhood.
And woman with motherhood,
with Christ teaching us to live in brotherhood.

The final bridge to cross is from life to the eternal realm,
with Christ Jesus at the helm.
But wait, there is another bridge to cross,
before we reach the cross.

We must cross the bridge of salvation,
there is no other conclusion.
For it is our transgressions,
when forgiven by Christ it gives new direction.

Salvation is a special bridge to cross,
Christ gave it to us on the cross.

Redemption for our soul to cleanse,
like the purity of a crystal lens.
Birth....to youth....to adulthood we all must pass.
Salvation...to Christian brotherhood...to Christ's
care we pass.
before we can reach the cross, without alas !

Christ helps us to cross the bridge to God's
eternal plan each day.
May God bestow His blessings on us each day.
The bridges of our life,
rest in God's Grace !
Through Him we are given new life,
then God we can embrace.

RG

GOD'S WHISPERING HOPE

The Holy Spirit is heaven's silent voice,
we hear it as our choice.
               Listen to the whisper.

We become God's guest,
received at our request
Listen to the whisper.

It touches our soul,
like winds gentle flow.
Listen to the whisper.

In solitude we hear the message,
recorded in the Good Book passage.
Listen to the whisper.

The whisper is an encompassing force,
for assurance reach for the source.
Listen to the whisper.

Daily through life we trod,
living by the grace of God.
Listen to the whisper.

God's whispering hope,
gives the faith to cope.
Listen to the "Whisper".

                                  RG

If we don't listen to God's whispering hope, then life is meaningless. And, if we don't believe that our soul is homeward bound, then faith is worthless and futile. Our purpose for living becomes a tragedy resulting in a dead end street, with Christ's promises being fruitless. It is our assignment and responsibility to draw attention to God's Word, which fulfills not only His precepts and promises, but

the interpretation of hymns sung and poems read. These all reflect the workings of the indwelling spirit. In other words "Christ's work" regardless of our inability to capture the full meanings and significance of "The Wonder of it All". Christ brought with Him "God's Whispering Hope" for all humankind. God's whispering hope was evident at Pentecost. It came in like the wind. That wind (spirit) has blown throughout humanity for over two thousand years. Christ's birth and death on the cross gave us salvation for the remission of sins. It is a covenant and promise. All is guaranteed in God's Word.

COME AND SEE

Come and see God's Holy Word;
story told throughout the centuries.
Hear of His power over humanity,
for He has sovereignty.
Abraham, Isaiah, and Moses tell the history,
those who came heard the story.

Come and see His name:
Jehovah - Jireh, "The Lord who provides."
The one who says, "Here I am", in me abide.
In your heart He should reside.

Jehovah - Rapho, "The Lord who heals."
To His sacrifice we should appeal,
grace and forgiveness He did reveal.
Through Him it becomes a redemptive deal.

Jehovah - Nissi "The Lord our banner."
Hold the flag of Christianity high in your walk,
telling others as you talk.
For He is in charge of our journey,
as told in the Epiphany.

Jehovah - Shalom, "The Lord is peace,"
Oh! In this world to find tranquility,
Shall it come only in eternity?

The Lord says "Do not fear, for I am here!".
Jehovah - T'sidkenu "The Lord our righteousness."
The prophecies were fulfilled on the cross,
Christ's wounds sealed our future as He paid the cost.
For He was God's Son, the righteous
through Him and only Him, otherwise we are scolded.
Jehovah - M'Kaddesh "The Lord our sanctifler."
On the cross crucified He hung, to our sinful ways he clung.

Then they were banished,
when His final act was finished.
For we are sanctified,
His elect to be justified.

Come and see Emmanuel "God with us".
A savior is born. His name is Jesus, as the story is told.
To the world a revelation will unfold.
As sentry, He stands at heavens gate,
checking the list and controlling our fate.
He is with us throughout each day,
for He is "God with us", a promise here to stay.
This is His Holy Spirit, always present,
till the day He comes in a glorious descent.

Come and see Jehovah - Sabaoth "The Lord Almighty."
The one who knows all things,
even before the beginning of time.
This the written proclaims,
His words thoughout history will chime.
Giving us hope and courage to the summit climb.
There a promise to live sublime.

Come and see "The faithful."
Those who give God the glory,
as we live and tell our own story.
For He is the commander,
He has the compass so that we don't get lost and wander.

Come and see and praise His name!
                                        RG

COME TO LIFE

Today, I sat in the woods,
thinking about God, as I should.
Listening to the brook,
as it wanders around each crook.

It was dark when I arrived,
then I waited to be surprised.
The trees took shape against the sky,
new leaves told me the reason why.
Wild flowers danced in the wind,
they told me the reason why.
The chirp of birds began to blend,
they told me the reason why.

Then the sun shone on new life,
then renewal came into my life.
For I had discovered the reason why,
to this my soul did reply.

God's spirit dwells everywhere as His choice,
we can't touch, see or hear His voice.
It is there always to which we awaken,
of which God's Word has spoken.

So it is to Christ's beckon,
that I now reckon.
Asking my sins to be forgiven,
For they have been my grieving.
For the spirit tells me the truth,
just as the Bible story told.

For the Bible is the Gospel truth,
it is to this revelation I now hold.
I shall trust in His way,
freeing me to have faith come what may.

Now I can "Cross the Bridge"
knowing that He will meet me on the other side
of the bridge.
Now I can water the morning glory,
and give Christ the glory.
Today I understand God,
along His path I shall trod.   RG

AWAKEN THY SOUL

Awaken ! God's Kingdom to reveal,
before His throne we should kneel.
To His Kingship pledge alliance,
in His Kingdom put your reliance.
His diety true and real,
your devotion do not conceal.

Welcome to God's promised land,
to enter shake His hand.
Enter with spirit sincere,
for He dwells near.
To our soul He giveth freedom,
free to enter God's Kingdom.

Awaken! God's word to hear,
a message we should revere.
A story told of God's presence,
to life surely there is relevance.
To our future it gives perspective,
acknowledge and be receptive.
The truth we can behold,
our spirit it will mold.

Awaken! Your soul in reverence,
before Him stand in attendance.
His Holiness is plainly clear,
His friendship, hold it dear.
Pray and send your conveyance,
let Him know your acceptance.
Your praises sing with zeal,
let Him know how you feel.

Awaken! Christ is our salvation,
victory over death was His crucifixion.
A crown of glory we shall wear,

He's our savior, we shall not fear.
Our redemption only through His assurance,
through Christ comes our deliverance.
To His forgiveness we appeal,
our soul's weakness He shall heal.

Awaken! Christ's love to portray,
from Christ's teachings we shouldn't stray.
To His unselfish love disciples testify,
through our love, His to exemplify.
Peace, joy, understanding, love does foster,
A loving bond will bring us closer.
Release it and watch it grow,
it will produce a radiant glow.

Give somebody a hug and transfer your love,
let it fly free like a dove.
Christ's love does the world surround,
loving peace in the world would abound.

Awaken! God's Kingdom to reveal.
Awaken! God's Word to hear.
Awaken! Your soul in reverence.
Awaken! God is our salvation.
Awaken! God's love to portray.
Awaken! The soul to God,
the cornerstone of life is God.
Forge ahead in full commitment,
fill your soul with contentment,
Unlock your soul,
enjoy the stroll.

RG

GOD'S BEACON OF LIGHT

In the distance I see a light,
its radiance is so bright.
The light, from where does it shineth ?
closer I look, Oh ! It's God's lighthouse.

His beacon is the direction to goeth,
my course steadfast plot. Destination? God's lighthouse.
Through life we must navigate,
many times in troubled state.

Some days our spirit glows with brightness,
other days, faced with darkness.
Our soul dampened with sadness,
desperately seeking happiness.

Our map of life needs rerouting,
a new course in the searching.
Remember God's beacon of light.
His light maketh all things right.
His light shines on the walkway of life,
no longer darkness, nor strife.

Use God's lighthouse to plot the course,
your bearing, beacon of the source.
Christ said "I am the way and the light"
set sail for God's beacon of light.
Destination is the glow of the light,
on arrival, open the door and see the light.
Your journey done in faithfulness,
your spirit, a heart of gladness.

RG

CHAPTER 4:

SPIRITUAL DEPRESSION

Romans 8:18 "I consider that our present sufferings are not worth comparing with the glory that will be in us."

Depression is a vicious enemy. It robs our spirit of happiness, it plagues us with discontent and it impedes our relationship with other people. It can carry over into our ability to perform effectively in our career. Many times the family suffers as well. It reaches the point where there has to be a resolve to tackle the issues that drag us down into what we perceive as a bottomless hole, a condition where we can't find the escape button to release us. We can't remove the barricade to our mental and spiritual well being.

Perhaps, the key to escape is the key that opens the window to "The Wonder of it All." Therein you'll find many surprises. Otherwise, we live for ever in the grasp of its demonic arms. It will control our destiny and our life. It requires identifying those issues that negatively impose on our will. Essentially, it is a fight with our will power to overcome the plague of thoughts that our minds harbor. Freedom is the ultimate goal, whether it being released to live with a clear conscience or a spiritual freedom in a positive and rewarding relationship with God. Freedom of expression is so important as it relates to revealing our identity, our wishes and our praise to our Creator for His boundless gifts. One will gain more insight to "God's world" as we develop a greater sense of gratitude for the blessings that come our way in life. However, reaching this point of satisfaction sometimes necessitates starting at square one as to what is causing our problem. It means untying the strangle-hold preventing us from living a life of spiritual freedom. Perhaps the best solution to approaching the inherent issues is to put pen to paper and make a list of the things you are dealing with. Perhaps you'll need to subdivide each topic to acquire a more thorough understanding of the circumstances.

In order for this process to be successful you must be completely honest with yourself. Even in the Bible God tells us to examine our motives, reasons and ambitions. There is a hymn that would be applicable to this pursuit. It is titled "Surrender All". That is extremely difficult when the person has lived with a spiritual deficiency for so many years. It can be very perplexing. A consolation is that we are not alone, thousands of people cope with this problem on a daily basis. The objective is to release it and get it out in the open, then closely examine each item of concern. It will surprise you how openness will help address the frustrations that perplex us. It is a matter of releasing the issues by dumping them into the river that flows to the "Lake of the Eternal Past." Many of our disappointment lie in the past. They are in the past and should not be a concern. That is one of the rewards of forgiveness. Such an approach will help us realize our purpose for living in Christ. At the same time it should build character and understanding which in return will reward us with a better perspective of the future. Knowing ourselves relative to the expectations of life gives us confidence, hope and assurance. We can walk into the future and face the challenges of tomorrow, for it is the power of the spirit that gives direction and freedom. To be in tune with Christ requires changes and modifications to our character. It will surprise you how openness will give the freedom to come to a resolve. Our spirit is up lifted. Knowing ourselves relative to the expectations of life gives us confidence, hope and assurance. We can walk into the future with an open mind. For it is the power of the mind and spirit that gives us direction. Direction leads to a new adventure.

Such is the case with this book and the collection of thoughts herein presented, an adventure full of discoveries, achievements, successes, happiness, etc. No longer held in bondage of that demonic enemy depression, thus giving us the freedom to explore further into "The Wonder of it all". I thoroughly realize that there are many ramifications to living with depression. This is particularly important when it impedes our spiritual well being, for our future depends on it. Dealing with it, for some people, requires many years of analysis to come to terms with it. It is an intrinsic part of life. A topic of concern to living a fruitful and joyous life. It behooves us a worthwhile study to probe into the relatedness and challenge to open the window and take a look at the many aspects of Christianity. Christian psychologists confirm that depressive thoughts can center around the invisibility of God and lack of faith. It under-mines the soul.

Perhaps the biggest mistake (sin) is not to try to rectify the situation. We allow ourselves to be lead down the path of failure and disappointment. That displeases God for He wants us to have life abundantly. Exploring the world of "The Wonder of it all" will yield some insights that make life worthwhile. The ingredients of a happy life vary from person to person. Each of us can pick out of the basket of 'The Wonder of it All" enough spiritual food to satisfy the appetite of all God's children, but we have to open the box, look in, and take out what we need. Although some people expect to much of themselves and end up with little. Or, in the case of salvation, nothing. Work ethics are important for achievement on earth. Work ethics for pleasing God is to magnify and multiply His Kingdom. He wants every human being to take advantage of His love, grace and mercy. Yet, despite His offerings people choose to live separate from Him. The result can be spiritual depression.

"With men it is impossible, but not with God: for with God all things are possible." (Mark 10:27,KJ) Perhaps the biggest stumbling block is that of not believing in ourselves. Quite often that is the result of comparing ourselves to other people, wanting to be just like a person we idolize. Then to not reach that goal can form a self-degrading complex with the attitude that I am insignificant or "I am worthless". Such thinking destroys self-esteem, many times resulting in living a life of inferiority and loneliness, even to the point that we feel a sense of rejection. I don't feel as though I am part of this group, perhaps wishing to escape from everything.

Escapism doesn't render a solution to the dilemma. The most important thing to realize is that God considers you a significant child of His domain. As a matter of fact, He will never cast you out. Why ? Because He sacrificed His Son's life for you. Don't be afraid to let go, allowing your imagination to dream of achieving that goal of freedom and the fulfillment of liberating dreams. Depression is an adversary. Yet, through positive thinking it can be eradicated, if not eliminated, at least fundamental ways to cope and keep its control in check. Get involved with doing good deeds, they will warm the heart. Don't be afraid to love others and don't compare yourself to others. God knows you just as you are. Remember the hymn "Just As I Am." Don't get into the habit of constantly putting yourself down. Let God lift you up. Develop a strength that you can rely on each morning, each day, and each night. Learn to take walks in the fields, the meadows, the forest, the mountains, and as you walk closely look at the creative genius of God, our heavenly Father. Become spellbound by His blessings and grace. The Bible tells us that much can be learned about the nature and generosity of God. Look at yourself, you are a miracle from the hands of our maker. Lastly, remember that our pain and suffering is minor compared to Christ's suffering on the cross. It is a matter of keeping your difficulties in perspective according to the wishes of Christ, our advocate.

"If God is for use who can be against us ?" (Romans 8:31, KJ) This is the frosting on the cake knowing that regardless of who we are He is always there to help us. All we have to do is dial 1-800-Jesus Christ. Remember he died for all our suffering, therefore, he is completely aware of our needs. He dwells with us each moment of each day of our lives. We have been granted the freedom to tap into that resource. He is the source of everything in the world and the spiritual realm as well. However, because of our shortsightedness, our pride, and our reluctance to change, we form a personal barrier and we become our own enemy. Yes, many times we are our own worse offender. This shows forth in our attitude and actions. God does not change, but we must be molded and become acceptable in His eyes. That should be the invitation and incentive to open the door wide to "The Wonder of it All" infusing that wonder into our mind and soul. Let God do His work !".

You may be weak in mind and spirit, but by expanding your knowledge of "The Wonder of it all" your soul will be nurtured, thus giving your life a renewed spirit and perspective. Not only faith in ourselves, but trust and confidence in what lies ahead. Not to look forward with anticipation is escapism. Not to charge forward with expectations is defeatism. Who wants to be a loser? It is the brave who face challenges in life. It requires mustering the fortitude to conquer the odds. Failure never won a battle. Initially, the battles won are small, but they provide the strength and courage to face bigger obstacles in life. The goal is to become independent in spirit, whether it be the spirit to charge ahead and/or whether it be the Holy Spirit giving us strength and direction. Actually, it is the combination of the two. For without God nothing is possible. With out Him life is a dead-end street. He is our scout. He left behind clues of how to make the journey. "If you abide in me, and my words abide in you, ye shall ask what ye will, and it shall be done unto you." (John 15:7, KJ) He has planted the seed in our soul and we harvest things more precious than Gold. It is finding these treasures that determines the measure of our faith. It is not something that is here today and gone tomorrow. ".....Lo, I am with you always, even unto the end of the world." (Matt. 28:20, KJ) "And not only this, but we exalt in our tribulations, knowing that tribulation brings about perseverance and perseverance proven character, hope; and hope does not disappoint, because the love of God has been poured out within our hearts through the Holy Spirit who was given to us." (Rom. 8:26-28, KJ) Perhaps the key word in this passage for those who attempt to dig themselves out of the pit of discouragement, what ever the case, is perseverance. God is simply saying "Don't give up!" Grab hold of imagination and inspiration. Grab hold of "The Wonder of it All."

God may be invisible today, but someday the light will shine on His Holiness for you. You'll develop the vision to see His grace. It is a must, for it determines our spiritual survival. Open the pages to your life and start writing new chapters. The things you'll discover in the "The Wonder of it all" will surprise you. An athlete can't win unless he/she prepares themselves for competition. That should be very obvious. Likewise with the Christian spirit, it requires flexibility in character and attitude to make changes to adapt to the expectations of God. It is not only a life-altering affair, it also is a necessary condition for eternal survival. Take a look at the history of mankind. Millions and millions of people have had to adjust and adapt to change. Many times there are dire consequences related to not making necessary modifications in our lives.

The switch of change must be turned on to find spiritual success and gratefication. That is the norm for everybody, so don't feel that you are any different. You have the same options open to you. He who doesn't explore doesn't find. He who doesn't look doesn't see. He who is blind gets lost. He who does not have courage always will fall short of expectations. A dream can not come to fruition unless there is hope. Without the proper spirit the road ahead becomes even more challenging and difficult. Sometimes hard knocks makes us stonger and gives us the determination to march on. Regardless of the circumstances, there will be a reward at the end of the path. Keep looking, there is hope to be found, treasures to be found and good friends to be found.

A DREAM CAN COME TRUE

Jesus said "If you canst believe, all things are
possible to him that believeth." (Mark 9:23KJ)

Through out life we have dreams,
often they come in a steady stream.
They are wishes to be fulfilled,
when they come true we are thrilled.

Though they may not come true now,
wait, be patient, wait for tomorrow.
Though obstacles my impede, be steadfast,
for a dream built on faith will last.

Often the road may be rough,
but to God pledge your oath.
The mind looks to the future,
with God planning the adventure.

When the dream comes true, Oh, the elation,
as we look to Jesus with anticipation.
Yes, our hopes and dreams will be tested,
but with perseverance dark shadows will be arrested.

For faith is a dream,
then believe with esteem.
For it is the courage in our hearts,
that makes the dream come true.

Dreams need to be nurtured,
to carry us into the future.

Finally, share your dream,
for together we are a team.

RG

KEEP ON TRYING

There is God's will and our will,
He expects us to try His will.
Our will can lead us astray,
compromising God's ways.

Yes, in life there are expectations,
challenges to face, some induce frustrations.
Sometimes we can't move forward,
then courage is the word.

Harboring hope each day,
to help carry us on the way.
What gives us strength in courage?
It is faith during such a passage.

For tomorrow depends on faith,
a spirit to keep on trying.
Trying keeps away defeat and despair,
then throw in a little prayer.
Trying keeps us on our journey,
Christ's promises is the reward.

For Christ said, in me you can trust,
as through life you thrust
So keep on trying,
and add a little singing.

RG

IN HIS CARE

In Christ we place our care,
as we look to the tomorrows.
In him it is a bonded affair,
for his grace we look afar.

Giving us courage for each step
we take, it is the knowing that instills hope.
A promise fulfilled, he did make,
a life line we can take.

So whatever transpires,
we are in his hands.
Such truth does inspire,
as we venture through his land.
Though we do not see the future,
he has a wonderful plan.

His spirit to us does nurture,
it prepares us for a new home..
Say yes to his offer,
for we'll be in his care.

It is a promise for us all,
for it is Christ who calls.
It is he who beckons us in his care.

RG

"Christ liveth in me;....by the faith of
of the Son of God, who loved me and
gave Himself for me." (Gal. 2:17)

THE MASTER'S HANDS

Oh universe from where did you come?
Planets, sun, moon, earth, stars,
Scientists, astronomers look afar.
Your work by them can't be explained.
Put there by the Master's hand.

Oh stars so beautiful in the night,
Your wonders fill my heart with delight.
Put in place by the Master's might.

Oh man from where did we come?
From organic-chemical soup, I think not!
From an ape did I evolve? Certainly not!
Body, heart, soul....brain, eyes, ears,
breathing, hearing, seeing, thinking.
Truly we are a marvelous thing.
Designed by the Master's mind.

Oh animals, from where did you come?
Your presence fills my soul with wonder,
dogs, cats, horses, elephants and deer.
Put there by the Master dear.

Oh birds, how graceful you soar,
your songs we adore.
Much you add to the out-of-doors.
Your flight built by the Master doer.

Oh flowers, you bloom with such beauty,
roses, tulips, daffodils, lily.
Your color, your fragrance on each adorned.
Painted in the Master's garden.

Of infant, miraculous to see you born
without you, we'd be forlorn.

Given to us and put in our care,
watching you grow, nothing can compare.
A present from the Master's hand.

Oh songs, music to the ears,
melodies that take away fears.
Filling life with cheers.
Life's discords singing away the tears.
Written by the Master who hears.
Oh God, where do you reside?
In the heavens far above?
Or in our hearts, dwelling inside?
Your presence put there by the Master's reside.

Oh Master so many gifts you give each day,
my gratitude I extend your way.
In church I must pray and give thanks.
Many blessings from the Master each day.

Oh Master, grant me the wisdom,
to have faith in thee.
You have a special kingdom especially for me,
wrought by the Master's hand.
Extend your hand I beseech thee,
that we shall walk hand-in-hand.
With the Master for eternity.

                                        RG

GOD IS NEAR

How do we know God is near,
as we daily go our way?

What possesses us to think He is there?
Or do we say he is here?

I see Him in all that surrounds,
I see Him in you and me.

Everywhere he abounds,
all we have to do is look and see.

In our hearts he is found,
to us he'll forever be.

To us he'll set the sails,
even when we are frail.

Yes, he is never far away,
united with every heart.

Trust in Him, day after day,
God is near and he'll never depart.

To this dream take hold,
for your faith he will mold.

RG

"The Lord is close to everyone who prays
to him. To all who truly pray to Him." (Psalm 17:6)

WAVES OF BLESSINGS

I sat on the seashore today,
looking at the horizon far away.
Where the blue sky meets the sea,
God's blessing of vision, so thankful to see.

Wondering where the waves come from,
all topped with white foam.
Their shapes cast against aqua green,
instilling a sense to relax and enjoy the scene.
Waves appear in abundant number,
one replaces the other in repetitious thunder.

I sat and watched as I slumber,
then these thoughts I remember.
God's blessings come from beyond the horizon,
Waves of blessings as life goes on.
Gracious gifts now to ponder.
To His grace we grow fonder.

The waves of life inherent to His creation,
for this we submit our adoration.
The waves of family and friends,
through us His spirit transcends.
A multitude of other waves in review,
as more waves come into view.

The wave of love as Christ makes His adoptions,
endless as the waves flow with constant motion.
Listen, hear and see the waves,
even though life's woes enslave.

Look to the horizon to see more,
as the waves roll to our shore.
So set on the beach reminiscing,
and count the waves of blessings.

Though the waves appear in restless artistry,
they instill a sense of pleasantry.
The curiosity to look beyond whence they came,
to God's mysterious majesty.

To give Him the fame,
and through His grace liberty.
When waves of blessings wash up on our shore,
give thanks more and more.

RG

THE RESTLESS SEA

The sea, the restless sea,
like life, its turbulence we can't flee.

On the rocks dreams are dashed,
some times in endless waves.
They burst onto the shore splashed.
Yet, their fulfillment the soul craves.

But wait, look to the horizon,
waves appear by the dozens.
Some destroy, others are good,
God tells us this should be understood.

Some are blessings, while from others we learn,
that counting our blessings carries us over the churn.
Shaping our faith, knowing God is in control.
Hang on to this as through life you stroll.

The sea gull flies above the turbulence,
wings spread and carried by the wind.
Reminding us of God's plan and His benevolence.
Keep forging those dreams and listen to the
"Whispering hope" of the wind.

The clouds above, though they dim our view,
see the sun, the Son "Christ" shines on the sea.
This is true !

With love,
Dad, August 2003

God in the Midst of Creation
With Us Each Dawning

CHAPTER 5:

IN THE WOODS WITH GOD'S GIFTS

MEMORIES IN REVIEW

Psalm 118:24 "This is the day the Lord has made;
let us rejoice and be glad in it"

This is the story of a young boy who well into his old age always enjoyed the outdoors. In his later years he recalls with pleasant recollection countless mental images of tracing those memories. They are a shinning example of how God can infuse blessings in the life of a person.

As you read on please recognize the fact that all these events did not transpire in one day. They are flashbacks to memories of the yesteryears. It is a continuous flow of pictures like on a slide projector set in motion. They induce a deep sense of gladness for simply having had the opportunity to experience them. What follows is a very quick march through those memories. All were made possible by God's creative majesty and the gift of life.

When I was a young boy, I always enjoyed the outdoors. Fishing a beautiful stream at the crack of dawn, casting a fishing line with bait or a lure into a pool of water below a rip, filled with the anticipation of a brook trout slamming the hook and the excitement of reeling in the evening dinner. But before placing it in the creel, admiring the beauty of the species.

Some of the best memories were times spent with my daughters and grand children, accompanied by my wife. Or, being awaken at 4:00 o'clock in the morning by the alarm clock. Then hurriedly eat breakfast and drive for an hour to my most favorite hunting spot. Then quietly walk into the woods to a tree stand or a ground blind. Then set with the anticipation of a large buck or torn turkey to pass by. The sun rises and glistens off freshly fallen snow, which causes the pine bows to bend. The snow covers the floor of the woods and fields with a white blanket. A blanket that has put the grasses, weeds and flowers to rest for the winter season.... Or, pack the camping gear and the family in a vehicle and head for a campground located on the sandy beach of a small lake with the Adirondack Mountains in the distance as a backdrop to our view across the lake. Then the next morning awaken to the coolness of a morning breeze and look across the lake to the eerie sight of fog lifting off the surface of the water. A day spent swimming, canoeing or fishing. At evening time close out the day by gathering around a camp fire talking and roasting marshmallows. Then come to the realization that the vacation has come to an end. Then, what seemed to be a long drive home. Yet, our minds were filled with fond memories. God had been good to us.

This day starts quietly, step by step, with as little commotion as possible, I enter the woods hoping not to disturb the deer or turkey, making every effort not to make the animals aware of my presence. I climb to a tree stand or enter a ground blind. Then I ready my equipment and sit back in a relaxed position to wait for the sun to poke its nose above the horizon. The trees are silhouetted against the morning sky. A torn turkey is heard gobbling from a large tree branch on a hillside across a brook that meanders through the meadow below, as if to say, "I am the alarm clock. Time to wake up wildlife!" Off in the distance the honking of geese are heard approaching, then in V-formation they glide overhead with grace in their wings. The lead goose seems to be beckoning, "follow me!" A fox scampers by looking for food and the pups sitting near the den begin barking from the hilltop. It appears that the birds heard the turkey and geese, for they now start chirping. The chickadees, blue jays, sparrows, cardinals and doves sing their melody, then burst into harmony. Some singing tenor, some soprano, others baritone and the crows sing bass. The orchestra of bird songs seem to give merriment to the squirrels as they scamper from branch to branch through the treetops performing aerial acrobatics. Then as though playing a game of chase, they chase each other around an oak tree, spiraling up and down the tree. It makes you dizzy watching them. A chickadee lands on my bow and arrow, then it looks at me as though to say, "Good Morning!" Later a wren takes perch on the brim of my hat, then flickers away. A chipmunk walks along the interwoven branches that make up the front of the blind, looks at me and says, "Have a great day!". A little deer mouse scurries through the undergrowth. On the other side of the meadow I sees a ten-point buck seducing a doe, then they wander off out of sight. A partridge flies in, the sound of its wing beat startles and alerts me. He lands on the other end of the log that I am is setting on, it walks along the log to within a few feet, then jumps down and walks over to my feet, then hops up on my shoe. I sit motionless to enjoy the moment. After a few seconds I loudly shout the word "BOO!". The startled bird instantly puts his wings into overdrive, leaving behind a bare spot were the leaves had been blown away. It then soars farther down the hillside to find a place where his life won't be disturbed by a human being. I imagine his heart beat was racing. Probably thinking "I've got to be more careful."

It is now time for a coffee break. The coffee is poured and cookies are taken from my lunch bag. It satisfies my desire for a morning snack. Motion on the far side of the meadow catches my attention. I quickly focuses my eyes to see a huge male coyote trotting along a deer trail that passes just below the ground blind. It is the first coyote I have ever seen in the wild. What a graceful animal! He passed by, crossed the creek and disappears in the hardwoods on the opposite hillside. An owl flies in, lands on a branch nearby and pronounces a few hoots. A hawk glides through the trees. The owl quickly departs, the squirrels and chipmunks scurrying to seek protection in their burrows. Three raccoons are seen climbing down from a hollow willow tree, walk across the meadow up a path and out of sight. A doe with two fawns cross the creek and appears on the right side of the meadow. They follow the stream and disappear in the brush. Shortly, thereafter, a doe walks in the front of the blind with a six- point buck following her. He, too, passes only seven yards away, so close that I almost could touch them. For deer it is the mating season. I also remember deer that have walked directly under my tree stand. I could look down and count every antler and watch muscles ripple as they moved.

Wow! What a cheerful morning. The food processor in my abdomen tells me that it is lunchtime. I lean up against an oak tree and partake of the sandwich and cookies I had packed the night before. While eating I am surrounded by all the birds singing in harmony. The serenity of the woodland setting and the soothing music of the birds puts me to sleep. How long I slept, I don't recall. I feel something nudge my foot and gradually open my right eye. To my amazement I see a doe sniffing my shoe. Upon opening both eyes and moving my head, the deer retreats a short distance to join another deer. They give me an inquisitive look. Their curiosity satisfied, they trot off.

After sitting for five hours, it is time to take a walk to limber up the muscles. I go in a direction away from the the hillside view of the meadow and follow a lane that descends to the bottom of the ravine. I look ahead and see another deer run up the ravine. Motion off to the left catches my eye. I see two buck fighting for territorial rights. One is an eight point and the other is a six point. They prance around studying each other, occasionally making bluff attacks. This goes on for about a half hour. Finally, the smaller buck decides that he isn't any match for the larger deer and he hurries up the stream bed with the other deer in hot pursuit. I now walk across the ravine to the stream. In doing so, I flush a small flock of mallard ducks. The iridescent green of the drakes head's show vividly in the sun light. The white collar around their necks and blue aft feathers add further to this spectacular view. Their departure leaves behind a slurry of patches on the surface of the water. I now cross the creek and climb the hillside to a rim that parallels the ravine. Once there, I quietly walk a few steps, stop, listen and study the woods. I do this for several hundred yards. Eventually I sees something, "Oh my gosh!" it's a doe giving birth to a fawn. What a magnificent opportunity to see this grand event. Thank you Lord!. I had observed the birth of animals before, but never in the wild.

I now walk through a thicket to the edge of a field. Looking ahead I see a rabbit bound into the brush. I then follow the field back to the edge of the ravine. Then I drop down to the bottom of the creek, cross it and head for another ground blind. Once there, I take off my backpack, open my folding seat and sit down to wait for more exciting views from natures showcase. I hear motion behind me. It is two deer dropping down to the bottom of the ravine, no more than thirty feet away. They mill around, gradually moving toward the stream, cross it and become lost in the hardwoods. A mink swimming down the creek crawls up the embankment a short distance away. He searches for food, then slithers back into the water. There are a few moments of silence, then up the ravine I notice dark objects moving through the brush. As they move closer I recognize a flock of turkey. Eventually they are directly in front of the blind. The flock consists of five toms. I have the pleasure of watching them scratch for food, chase each other, stand on a log and flap their wings. One even spreads his tail feathers in full display. Another reward for being in the woods with God's gifts.

The sun is starting to drop toward the horizon, signaling that it is time to pack and head for home. As I walk through a field on my way to the car, I flush a pheasant. This immediately causes me to recall the many times I went pheasant hunting over the years. I remembers the dogs I hunted with, especially Barney Boy, an Irish Setter. What a joy it was to watch him flush a bird and retrieve it. He would bring it to me with exceptional pride. Barney would drop the bird at my feet and look up at me with an expression, "I have pleased you master and I love you." I would reward him with a few pats and say either "Shall we find another pheasant?" or "Shall we go home?" Oh, how Barney enjoyed running in the fields looking for birds. Many a dinner meal was served with savory pheasant on the platter. As I drove away from the woods I look back and say, "Thank you for these fond memories." I then drive toward the west into the setting sun. A celestial artist has painted the sky with a blend of pink, orange and red. What a delightful way to end the day spent with God's Gifts in the woods.

On the way home I pass by many lakes and streams I had fished over the years from a boat or fishing through the ice in the winter. My mind is filled with many memories of catching fish. It prompts me to reflect on those special episodes in my fishing experiences. One of the occasions was with a teacher friend who owned a four seater Cessna airplane. On one occasion we flew to where the ski jump is now located a short distance south of Lake Placid in the Adirondack Mountains of New York State. We landed in a hay field landing strip and spent two days fishing the east branch of the Ausable River. Seventeen trout were caught the first afternoon. Another fond memory was a fishing trip into the backcountry north east of Truo, Nova Scotia. I had been appointed by the N.Y.S. Education Dept. to teach two graduate level courses on an extension basis at Dalhousie University in Halifax, Novs Scotia. One of the students in the class invited me to go trout fishing. On a Saturday morning, at about six o'clock, he picked me up. we drove about two hours to reach pur destination. After driving a few miles through a forest of huge pine trees we came to a meadow over looking a brook. Gathering our fishing tackle, we walked another two miles to an old abandoned saw mill. Beyond the mill was a brook. After pushing through dense alder bushes, we saw a sight to behold. It was a huge beaver dam about ten feet high and two hundread feet long. The water was back-up for about a quarter mile. The two of us stood on top of the dam in amazement, filled with awe at this magnificent work accomplished by a small animal known as the beaver. I peered into the pristine crystal clear water and said, "Look at the weeds swaying back and forth at the bottom of the pond." The student replied, "Sir, those are cutthroat trout swimming around, thousands of them." I was spellbound and speechless. Then we ventured into the activity of catching trout. My student caught over seventy and I caught about fifty. At one point a doe moose snuck up behind me. I was amazed at the curiosity of the animal. This spectacular experience was a very special moment in my out of door adventures.

Another special moment was when our family was camping at a favorate campground. I arose early in the morning to fish a nearby reservoir. At that time I was fishing with a square stern canoe propelled by a 2hp outboard Johnson motor. I motored out to deep water, lowered my copper line over the side and started trolling. With in minutes I caught a lake trout, then another and the third one, which is the creel limit. Within forty-five minutes I was back at my vehicle, loaded the canoe and went back to join my family at the campground. The trout dinner at super time was delicious. The only other story that might rival this one is when I and my son-in-law were fishing (trolling) Lake Ontario for king salmon. By ten thirty in the moring we had caught seven kings raning from 28 lbs to 35 lbs. a catch never to be repeated again. Behold, "The Wonders of Gods gifts".

At home I have a den with trophy antlers and pictures hanging on the walls. There is a desk at which to write, bookshelves, a gun cabinet, and a soft armchair. I often would sit and replay those memories of camping, fishing and hunting. Camping with my wife and daughters are filled with many happy times together. I and my wife did at one time own an old mobile home on the St. Lawrence River, where we had the pleasure and excitement of watching our grandchildren catch and reel in fish. What a pleasure it was to watch the expression on their faces. Then one of them would say "Grandpa, look at what I caught? Mine is bigger than yours, Ha! Ha!

Back to the woods. There is something special about the serenity, the quietude, the beauty and the peacefulness that wildlife instills while sitting in the woods with God's gifts. By now you have probably formed the question, "Why have I revealed these special memories?". It is to draw attention to the fact that I, as well as many thousands of people, take for granted the Gifts of God. We use Gods creation as a playground, then forget to tell Him "Thank You!" Reminiscencing helps to put life experiences in perspective. Sitting in the woods provided a lot of time to reminisce, especially to think about our Creator and other aspects of life. Because of past circumstances, I regarded nature and wildlife as my church, yet could never find my Lord. I developed the philosophy that God created all these wonderful gifts. Therefore, I formed the idea that I should be able to understand the mysteries of God's nature and establish a relationship with Him in the woods. Later in life, the need to accomplish this objective became a pressing issue. It ultimately intensified to the point where I was experiencing serious moods of depression. The woods became my sanctuary to internalize a correlation between God's gifts, the Bible, prayer, faith, and the compounded realities of life. I restored to writing poetry to express my gratitude for God's Gifts of creation. In a sense, they were prayers. Prayers recognizing the wonders of God's work, but also, prayers to earnestly seek God's attention. Prayers which I thought fell on deaf ears because there wasn't a Holy Spirit responding to say "I hear you!". There was an ever present desire to find God and determine why I had a continued sense of rejection by Him. This set the stag for a lengthy struggle searching and probing to find a relationship with my Creator. To hear His voice, to see a vision or feel His touch. The continuation of the stories to follow reveals a journey to find our Lord, Christ Jesus.

I was always awed by the wonder of the many forms of life on earth, especially human life. All the gifts of God and the influence they have on our daily lives leaves us filled with great wonderment, to the point that we can't comprehend, nor express in words to make any sense or understanding. It is beyond our ability to utter an appropriate "Thank You!" Yet it is our duty to delight in God's wonderous gifts.

"The earth is the Lord's and everything in it." (Psalm 24:1, KJ)

"When I consider Your heavens, the work of Your fingers.
The moon and the stars which you have ordained.
You have made him (man) to have dominion over the works of Your hands.
You have put all things under his feet." (Psalm 104, KJ)

"You are worthy, O Lord",
to receive glory and honor and power,
For You created all things,
and by Your will they exist and were created." (Rev. 4:11, KJ)

"Who has measurerd the waters in the hollow of His hand, measured heaven with a span, and calculated the dust of the earth in a measure?
 Weighted the mountains in scales, and the hills in a balance."
(Isaiah 40:12,KJ)

"He hath made the earth by His power, he hath established the world by his wisdom, and stretched out the heavens by his understanding."
(Jer. 51:15,KJ)

"For by him were all things created, that are in heaven, and that are on earth, visible and invisible." (Col.,KJ)

"Be thou exalted, O God, above the heavens; let thy glory be above all the earth." (Psalm 57:5.KJ)
"And, thou Lord, in the beginning hast laid the foundation of the earth; and the heavens are the works of thine hands." (Heb. 1:10,KJ)

I WONDER

I wonder at the glorious sunrise,
yes, even a beautiful sunset
Awaken each day with God to rise.
The peace that He will inward set.

I wonder at clouds drifting by,
and, the bluish hue of the sky.
The stars at night, glittering bright,
celestial bodies in a universe vast.
On earth our being, He cast.
Life, a gift from distant past.

I wonder at nature which surrounds,
where wildlife abounds.
Thank God with great resound.
The flowers, the birds, the animals,
the wonder they bring.
Their beauty endless like a spring.

I wonder at the new born infant,
the miracle of its first breath.
A body living in an instant.
A wonder beyond comprehensions breath.

I wonder as a child grows,
good health, good deeds as well.
Will his love on others bestow,
rightly doing God's Will.

I wonder at each persons soul,
each person different inward and out
Yet, each serving a special role,
created by God, yet His name they won't shout.

I wonder at man's genius,
the comforts he has wrought
God endowed, then given to us,
all things through Him sought.

I wonder at the deity of Christ,
His teachings, his everlasting promise.
Death denied by the risen Christ,
His salvation we should not dismiss.

I wonder at eternal life,
when faith is put to the test.
Knowing death is heavens gateway.
Assurance of Christ's saving grace on that day.

I wonder at God's plan,
in a world, tragedy filled.
He leadeth me through life's span,
His spirit, eternal hope instilled.

Jesus said, "Never cease to wonder."
not to wonder, is a spiritual dead.
Continue to wonder and forge ahead,
with God your soul to be lead.

In faith forever wonder,
your future, rejoice and ponder.
Live the endless dream,
flowing as an endless stream.

RG

GOD'S CREATIVE GENIUS

Each morning we admire a new show.
The Master Artist has painted another day.
It causes our spirit to bow,
for His genius sent our way.
It gives us the inspiration to start another day,
and say a fervent prayer.
Thank Lord for another day.
Sometimes I forget to give praise,
busy hands and minds causes our delay.

We appreciate the beauty of your design,
for it supports life and gives us pleasures.
You gave us life with this special gift,
it gives us fulfillment as we count our treasures.
For it tells us you really care,
made for us, your children.

We express gratitude for this earthly sphere,
may our thoughts be heard by your ear.
Oh, the power of your genius,
for you have been so good to us.

Each day is a surprise,
as each morning we arise.
Yet, knowing you we shouldn't be surprised.
If I forget to say "Thank you!",
just send me another flower as a reminder.

                                                                RG

"He has made His wonderful works to be
remembered." (Psalm 111)

THE MASTER'S HANDS

Oh universe from where did you come?
Planets, sun, moon, earth, stars,
Scientists, astronomers look afar.
Your work by them can't be explained.
Put there by the Master's hand.

Oh stars so beautiful in the night,
Your wonders fill my heart with delight.
Put in place by the Master's might.

Oh man from where did we come?
From organic-chemical soup, I think not!
From an ape did I evolve? Certainly not!
Body, heart, soul....brain, eyes, ears,
breathing, hearing, seeing, thinking.
Truly we are a marvelous thing.
Designed by the Master's mind.

Oh animals, from where did you come?
Your presence fills my soul with wonder,
dogs, cats, horses, elephants and deer.
Put there by the Master dear.

Oh birds, how graceful you soar,
your songs we adore.
Much you add to the out-of-doors.
Your flight built by the Master doer.

Oh flowers, you bloom with such beauty,
roses, tulips, daffodils, lily.
Your color, your fragrance on each adorned.
Painted in the Master's garden.

Of infant, miraculous to see you born
without you, we'd be forlorn.

Given to us and put in our care,
watching you grow, nothing can compare.
A present from the Master's hand.

Oh songs, music to the ears,
melodies that take away fears.
Filling life with cheers.
Life's discords singing away the tears.
Written by the Master who hears.
Oh God, where do you reside?
In the heavens far above?
Or in our hearts, dwelling inside?
Your presence put there by the Master's reside.

Oh Master so many gifts you give each day,
my gratitude I extend your way.
In church I must pray and give thanks.
Many blessings from the Master each day.

Oh Master, grant me the wisdom,
to have faith in thee.
You have a special kingdom especially for me,
wrought by the Master's hand.
Extend your hand I beseech thee,
that we shall walk hand-in-hand.
With the Master for eternity.

RG

HE'S GOT THE WHOLE WORLD IN HIS HANDS

He's got the whole world in His hands,
He's got the wind and the rain,
He's got the tiny little baby,
He's got you and me, brother, sister.
He's got the whole world in His hands.

FOR ALL THESE THINGS

From mountain heights and vaulted skies,
Your hand is clearly seen;
We cast our praise with natures cry.
For promises from age to age,
That caused our hearts to dream;

Purest adoration we impart.
From ransomed men of tender heart,
Whose souls You taught to sing;
Your children lift their voice to You.

For refuge from the darkening storm,
and rest beneath Your wings;
We worship You with grateful hearts.
With thanks for all these things!

The Celebration Hymnal

THIS IS MY FATHER'S WORLD

This is my Father's world.
And to my listening ears,
all nature sings and round me rings,
The music of the spheres.

I rest me in the thought of
rocks and trees and skies and sea.
His hand the wonders wrought.
The birds their corals raise;

The morning light, the Lily white,
declare their Maker's praise.
He shines in all that's fair,
In the rustling grass, I hear Him pass.
He speaks to me everywhere.

The Celebration Hymnal

HOW GREAT THOU ART

O Lord, my God, when I awesome wonder,
consider all the worlds Thy hands have made,
I see the stars, I hear the rolling thunder,
Thy power thro-out the universe displayed,

When thro' the woods and forest glades I wander,
and hear the birds sing sweetly in the trees.
When I look down from lofty mountain grandeur,
and hear the brook and feel the gentile breeze;
Then sings my soul, my savior God, to thee;
How great thou art!

FOR THE BEAUTY OF THE EARTH

For the beauty of the earth,
For the glory of the skies,
For the love which from our birth,
Over and around us lies;

For the wonder of each hour,
Of the day and of the night,
Hill and vale and tree and flowers,
Sun and moon and stars of light;

For the joy of human love,
Brother, sister, parent, child,
Friends on earth and friends above,
For all gentle thoughts and mild;

For thyself, best gift divine,
To our race so freely given,
For that, great love of Thine,
Pease on earth and joy in heaven.

The Celebration Hymnal

LET ALL THINGS NOW LIVING

Let all things now living,
a song of thanksgiving to the creator triumphantly raise;
Who fashioned and made us,
protected and stayed us,
Who still guides us onto the end of our days.

God's banners are over us.
His light goes before us,
A pillar of fire shinning forth in the night.
Till shadows have vanished,
and darkness is banished,
As forward we travel from light into light.

His law He enforces;
The stars in their courses,
and seen in its orbit abundantly shine.
The hills and the mountains,
the rivers and fountains,
The depth of ocean proclaims Him divine, Alleluia !

We, too, should be voicing,
our love and rejoicing;
With glad adoration a song let us raise.
Till all things now living,
unite in thanksgiving,
"To God in the highest, honor and praise."

The Celebration Hymnal

LORD, THANKS FOR THE GIFTS

Lord, you bestowed on us bountiful gifts,
They lift our spirit in our earthly life.
So often we take for granted your treasures,
We fail to see in fullest measure.

The ways that you care for us,
Your provisions, there shouldn't be any excuse.
Around the world we see your creation,
Our survival depends on those provisions.

You are like a fountian,
With blessings flowing in continous motion.
Yes, you are the Father who cares,
For there is no other to compare.

You feed the multitudes,
We should respond with gratitude.
Your art gallery is in full display,
The beauty you send our way.

You gave us life, ours to have and behold,
Why? Your love we are told.
Yes, sometimes we complain,
Tarmishing your gifts with stain.

Help us to understand,
So we can praise you for this land.
You own the fields, the woods and the birds,
The animals, the flowers and the sea.

All done in your name,
We must give you the fame.
                              RG

Hurray, It's Spring Time

CHAPTER 6:

HURRAY ! IT'S SPRING TIME

Spring flowers nudging through the soil,
reaching for life, an endless toil.
Searching for the sun rays,
shinning from far away.

Buds appear with anticipation,
bursting forth in full expectation.
Crocus and tulips radiant glow,
to our senses vividly flow.
Daffodils with golden hue,
giving us another clue.

Brilliant colors fill the garden,
God's paint brush from days of Eden.
An artistry beyond compare,
as through window I stare.

Even the trees sway in prelude,
a season they shan't elude.
Each leaf extended like a hand,
gathering light as God planned.

The arrival of the bluebirds,
and, songbirds I have heard.
Lawns turn a vibrant green,
all part of this glorious scene

Birds flicker about with grass in their beak,
at the birdhouse they stop to peek.

A freshness in the air,
ushering in a special affair.

In our souls a spirit surrounds,
could it be spring that abounds?
Revival of hope each morning,
that there is a new dawning.
God's signposts for our reading,
to have faith and keep reaching.

RG

Why the flowers nudged through the soil:
"So Jesus said to them....if you have faith as a grain of mustard seed,
nothing will be impossible unto you." (Matt. 17:20, KJ)
"....for by faith you stand." (2 Cor. 1:14, KJ)
"....the steadfastness of your faith in Christ." (Col. 2:5, KJ)

WINTER TO SPRING

As the seasons change there is a lesson to be learned,
for God is in nature at every turn.

God displays His creative genius,
designed especially for us.

Like magic winter puts the fields to rest,
dormant plants lay in winters nest.

The bleakness tests our hope,
but patience gives us strength to cope.

Plants are asleep for a special reason,
ready to sprout forth in their season.

Then in great triumph they appear,
beauty abundant as through windows we peer.

Now spring before us lay,
God's artistic gallery on display.

Oh, the heartfelt glory it enthralls,
helping us to in God stand tall.

For He has blessed us with a lesson,
the beauty of a Christian spirit as we plod on.

For we, too, will experience a change in season,
for the spring reminds us of renewal and rebirth of our soul.

For spring is a treasure,
if we grasp it in fullest possible measure.

RG

SMILE LITTLE FLOWER

I watched as a flower broke through the soil,
it had met the challenge of toil.
Then it opened its face with a smile,
reaching for the sun, to bask in its warmth for awhile.
Its face filled with radiant color,
revealing its faith to grow taller.

Its smile fills the air with joy,
so that others can enjoy.
Helping others to fulfill their dream,
as they flow along life's stream.
So it is with each person,
to understand the reason.

Even thought we toil, we'll emerge,
looking to the "SON" for our souls to purge.
Then on our face wear a smile,
knowing he'll go the extra mile.
Show forth a smile like the little flower,
then as we travail, over our troubles we can tower.
Smile little flower giving us hope in Christ's power.

RG

Why the flower smiles:
Galatians 5:22 "But the fruit of the Spirit is love, joy...
Galatians 2:20 "I live by the faith of the Son of God"
Luke 15:10 "....I say to you, there is joy in the presence
 of the angels of God over one sinner who repents....

Flowers and fresh green leaves remind us of new life (rebirth) in
the sights and pleasantries of springtime. Paul said "The human heart
can know God through the handiwork of nature (creation). To God

we are a seed planted and fertilized by the Holy Spirit. We blossom like a spring flower. We experience the same analogy through Jesus Christ (rebirth). It becomes the spring time in our personhood. The flowers reach for the celestial sun and we reach for the Son, Jesus Christ. Thank you spring for the reminder.

FOR THE BEAUTY OF THE EARTH

For the beauty of the earth,
For the glory of the skies,
For the love which from our birth,
over and around us lies;
Lord of all, to thee we raise,
this our hymn of grateful praise.

For the wonder of each hour,
of the day and of the night,
Hill and vale and tree and flower,
sun and moon and stars of light.

For the joy of human love,
brother, sister, parent, child;
Friends on earth and friends above;
for all gentle thoughts and mild.

Lord of all, to thee we raise,
this our hymn of grateful praise.

The Ladder Of Faith

CHAPTER 7:

FAITH

Romans 12:3 "....as God has dealt to
everyone a measure of faith."

What is faith ?

1. How do we define it ? It is invisible, only to be seen in action.
    The Holy Spirit is invisible, yet we see in each individual person
    the influence of the indwelling spirit.
2. Faith, hope and trust are to some degree synonymous.
3. Faith is the expectation of things to come. The invisible come
    true.
    Examples: a. Growth of a continued marriage bond built around
    love.
    b. The trust of a child in his/her parents.
    c. Hope in things not yet experienced or seen.
    d. Faith in salvation is the process by which we
    resurrect our separation from God to reach a point
    of intimacy.
    e. Hymn writers: All sinners, yet composed the lyrics
    of countless songs of praise. What was the driving
    force compelling and assisting them to write hymns
    ? It was faith that provided the impetus to bring
    forth words of conviction from the heart.

Christ reveals and promises salvation through his redemptive
powers. That is the essence of the Christian faith. All the other aspects
of this belief are the result of a transformation taking place in attitude,
conduct, and actions. For some people there is a misconception about
what constitutes genuine faith. It isn't an injection of some magical

substance that automatically transforms a person. It isn't as simple as that. As with all educational principles and disciplines, it takes time to comprehend what it is all about. Too often a person commits him/herself before fully realizing the consequences of making that choice. Thorough preparation of a person is paramount before walking with Christ. That is why some churches require a person to attend confirmation classes. Understanding should always precede entering into a relationship with a divine authority. In other words, it is a growing process. It should be a binding with our Lord. It takes time to manifest Christ like maturity. As a matter of fact, it is impossible. It can be our nemesis if we don't understand the forgiving nature of Christ. Why, because we alone can never reach the purity and beauty of a Christ like maturity. This is where we let God do His work. Each person develops according to an individual sense of commitment and understanding. It is the Word of God and the Holy Spirit of Christ dwelling within and guiding us. It is a spiritual frame of mind attempting to get "Nearer to my God to thee" (hymn). For some people it is a long arduous task. Why ? Personal prejudices, pride, misconceptions, resistance and the fact that the Holy realm is beyond our comprehension. Our deeds, conduct and works reflect the assimilation (conversion) of a Christ like attitude. When inspirational thoughts well up from the well spring of our soul, we then realize and know that the Lord has given us a special gift. When you see an infant born or a flower blossom realizing that it is the creative genius of God.

"Lo, I am with you always, even unto the end of the world." (Matt. 28:20, KJ) Hebrews 13:5 "Never will I leave you, nor will I forsake you." (Heb. 13:5, KJ) These are words directly from the lips of Jesus. He was the Son of God and He was granted full authority over our salvation. How can we with a clear conscience dispute such a claim. To believe means we have faith in those words not only in a contractual sense but in a loving heart to heart commitment. Otherwise, our fate for life beyond the grave is futile. Through salvation we are permitted by God to walk with Jesus until the end of the age. Our earth, as we know it today, will someday come to an end. The end of the age means life will not exist as we know it today. The only hope we have for continued life is through Jesus Christ's love, grace and mercy when he, and only he, grants redemption and everlasting life. Then we are promised exemption from the judgment seat of God. We by-pass that event. Our salvation will never be subject to foreclosure. The covenant we have through Jesus will never be nullified or void. Why ? Because God is faithful in His offering of redemption. "I am the resurrection, and the life: he who believeth in me will live, though he were dead, yet he shall live." (John 11:25, KJ) Remember, he is the Holy and Perfect One. He will never fail us or lie to us. Commitment to this philosophy is called "Faith." Faith is fine tuning our conscience to God's expectations. And, faith leads to "The Wonder of it all". Memorizing scripture or going to church does not give us eternal life. Keep it simple, it's the "Faith"! Faith radiates from the heart. Adopting what Jesus said "I am the way and the life". So study Jesus and you'll discover faith in its purest form and maturity. Try to avoid one big pit fall or misconception, some people try to convince us that once we receive the grace of his forgiveness our troubles will disappear. We still will encounter the struggles of the human race. However, through forbearance and faith we can rise above our trials and tribulations. In life we have two choices. To live life separated from God or join Him in a united effort to please our Heavenly Father. Deuteronomy 30:19 "I have set before you life and death.....therefore choose life, that you and your descendants may have life. (Deu. 30:19JKJ) Life is not a dead end street. Sir Walter Scott said, "Is death the last step ?." "He that beleiveth on the Son hath everlasting life." John 3:36,KJ) Emily Matthews said "Don't be afraid to dream". Faith is a dream being nurtured daily by the Holy Spirit of Christ. Jesus said "Verily, verily, I say to you, unless one is born anew, he can not see the Kingdom of God. (John 3:3, KJ)

How do we identify spiritual and/or inspirational faith. A blind lady during the late 1800's and early 1900's wrote 9,000 hymns. Her name was Fanney Crosby. She was filled with the spirit of the grace of Jesus. There are the hymn writers of the past. All sinners, yet composed the lyrics of countless songs that we sing in church today to worship our Creator. It was faith that provided the impetus to bring forth convictions of the heart.

John 14:6 "I am the way, the truth and the life".

Faith could be considered an investment plan in the future. Faith is the honey on the bread of life that gives us a smooth journey. It lubricates our emotions and expectations-Faith is absorbing God's grace and love. It determines who we are in Christ. A sponge absorbs water and releases it for a purpose. The leaves of trees and other plants by osmosis absorbs sun light and converts its energy to support itself. Essentially, our Christ like transformation is revealed through our faith. Faith being a composite of many things that supports our spiritually. Genuine faith gives us strength, courage, perseverance, hope and a glad heart. In order to please God, faith must be active, not passive. God commands us to be witnesses and disciplines in His name. Hoping, in part, to reflect His image. Thus living a purpose driven life reflective of our gratitude for salvation. All part of the philosophy that God out of his generosity granted us an abundant life, with salvation making life more abundant Therefore, he requests that we return a portion of our blessings. Thus, preventing us from not becoming greedy for the benefit of all His children. Behold, "The Wonders of Faith". A person could say that faith is "The Heartbeat of Christianity".

THE LADDER OF FAITH

I see a ladder I can climb,
a special ladder, one rung at a time.
The ladder is named FAITH.
Each rung spells F-A-I-T-H.

"F"   stands for HEAVELY FATHER;
        God reaching with gentle hand.
        His help leads me one step further.
        For my soul on which to stand.
        Forever, the Heavenly Father.

"A"   stands for God's AFFECTION;
        His love forever unceasing,
        a love with great compassion.
        My soul forever reaching,
        forever seeking His affection.

"I"   stands for His INSPIRATION;
        The strength to carry on each day.
        A life filled with satisfaction,
        Truly, there is no other way,
        Guided by His inspiration.

"T"   stands for THANKFULNESS;
        Life abounds with blessings,
        how often we forget His graciousness,
        In prayer we keep asking,
        don't forget to have thankfulness.

"H"   stands for HOPE;
        Hope gives courage for tomorrow.
        to face life's sorrows,
        With Christ's tutelage, we try to cope,
        faith gives birth to hope.
        The cross, Christ's resurrection,
        hope fulfilled by salvation.

The LADDER OF FAITH, we steadfast climb,
there to find Christ in time.

                        RG

THE SWALLOWS NEST

This morning I watched swallows build a nest,
one piece at a time, then the next and the next.
So diligent in their task,
in anticipation, if you should ask.

In hurried fashion they make preparation,
to add new life to God's creation.
They give a birth as their reward,
as time marches onward.

Atop the birdhouse they chirp a merry tune,
knowing that a special gift will arrive soon.
So it is with our faith,
built one piece at a time,
with patience and endurance ascending the climb.

But remember, faith needs constant repair,
prayer to our Lord, Christ Jesus, our struggles he'll share.
For He promises a reward,
if our faith makes us worthy to march onward.

Jesus said, I prepare a nest,
it is up to you to do the rest.
It is in heaven that we build our nest,
for it is there we'll find rest,

In heaven lay up your treasures,
with gladness in your hearts to the fullest measure.
Thank you swallows for building a nest,
for you helped me to understand the rest.
Now I can live life to my very best,
each day building a nest.

RG

Jesus said "I go to prepare a place for you," (John 14:2, KJ) "Lay up your selves treasures in heaven......for where your treasure is there will your heart be also." (Matt. 6:20,21,KJ)

2 Timothy 2:12 "If we endure, we will also reign with Him." (2 Tim. 2:12,IBML)

Hebrews 11:1 "Faith is the substance of things hoped for." (Heb. 11:1,IBML)

O LORD, FERTILIZE MY SOUL

Plant the seed of wisdom,
so that I understand your Kingdom.
For it is there we find freedom.

Plant the seed of wonder,
so that I search and ponder.
So that to You I grow fonder.
Plant the seed of appreciation,
so that I don't take for granted your creation.
For there we find sustenance and fruition.

Plant the seed of patience,
so that I can stand firm in my reference.
And, stand with you in obedience.

Plant the seed of liberty,
to praise you with certainty.
A song to express with gayety.

Plant the seed of clarity,
so that there I find serenity.
Giving life more vitality.

Plant the seed of charity,
for there are many in need.
They wait for a benevolent deed.

In my soul plant the cross of Jesus,
To stand steadfast and behold His gift to us.
So that in Him we can trust,
and not into evil be thrust.

Lord, fertilize these seeds,
this wish I plead.
Fill my spirit with faith,
for you are the source which nobody else hath.

RG

TO SEE WE NEED A VISION

Faith is developing a vision to see the Holy Spirit in our lives. Whether it is shown forth in God's creative genius or the influence it has on peoples lives, it is always there and alive. How do we develop a vision of an invisible God? God's love and care for us is by way of the spirit. Like the wind that fills the sails of a boat propelling it onward. We can't see it, but when the wind stops blowing, it disappears. Like love it is invisible. Yet, we feel it in our hearts. We sense it when people greet us, write a letter or we receive a get-well card in the mail. Our emotions can be stirred by it. All this gives a vision of the presence of love. God's word to us in the Good Book accomplishes the same emotions and assurance. Our vision of Chrit's love is formed by piecing together clues from the Bible, especially the New Testament. If we use our imagination, we can see God's (Christ's) love in action. A spirit that propels us forward and onward to face all the tomorrows and the will to promote good-will. It is the fuel that guides us to a destination promised by Jesus.

To gain further insight to our vision of God's Kingdom, please turn in a hymnal to the hymn "Be Thou My Vision." By reading it you will discover some clues that when internalized influences our thinking that helps to form an image or vision of Christ to us. It establishes to some degree the nature of God and all he offers. It further suggests that by a Christian birthright we have an inheritance to that vision. When developed it instills in us joy and hope to build our faith on. This vision should be harbored in our hearts, minds and souls as we progress through life. For we see God's truth in a new dimemsion. It declares us as son's and daughter's of our heavenly Father. We develop an appreciation for this vision. For we come to the conclusion that He is our creator in heaven. In closing, it admonishes us to realize that He is our King in heaven and Master of all things. we are truely indebted.

HYMN: OPEN MY EYES THAT I MAY SEE

Open my eyes that I may see,
glimpses of truth Thou hast for me;
Place in my hands the wonderful key,
that shall unclasp and set me free.

Open my ears that I may hear,
voices of truth, Thou sendest clear:
And while the wave notes fall on my ear,
everything false will disappear.

Open my mouth and let me bear,
gladly the warm truth everywhere;
Open my heart and let me prepare,
love with Thy children there to share.

The Celebration Hymnal

I ASK ONE PLEA

Lord, I ask one plea,
Your domain vast as the seas.
My preponderance, your love and grace to see.

Fill this heart of mine,
Your spirit infuse at this time.
To your image I shall climb,
let the spirit to heaven sing and chime.

Your breath to my soul adhere,
a message bright and clear.
Hope to the future as I peer,
Your presence and promises I hear.

My hand please clasp,
guiding each step of the way.
Your love and grace attached to me like a hasp.
A divine harmony that will last.
Let it be on this day.

RG

SEND ME YOUR SPIRIT

Lord, send me your Spirit,
Let my heart feel it.
Your grace unit with me,
For I want to please thee.

Instill in me your love to give me faith,
Guide me along your Kindom's path.
So that I can find thee.
And, know that it is free.

Let Christ, my will subdue,
So that I know what to do.
Send me his spirit today and always,
Let it dwell day after day.

RG

Faith means being sure of things we hope for and know that something is real, even if we do not see it.

"But without faith it is impossible to please Him. (Heb. 11;6 KJ)

Mark 9:23 KJ "All things are possible for the one who believes." This is essentially saying "If I can." It is will power and faith that says "I will."

Hymn: Be still and know that I am God.
         I am the Lord that healeth me.
         I love you with a steadfast love.

Hymn: Be still, my soul! The Lord is on thy side;
         Leave to the God to order and provide;
         To guide the future as He has the past.
         All known mysterious shall be bright at last.
         His voice who ruled them while He dwelt below.

John 14:1 KJ "Let not your heart be troubled; ye believe in God, beleive in me" When troubles knocks at our door....be happy that you are sharing in Christ's suffering so that you will be happy and full of joy when Christ comes in."

In comparison we can never suffer to the degree that Christ did. Also, look around and you'll find countless numbers who are suffering greater tragedies than we. Such tribulations are there to test the strenght of our faith.

HYMN: BREATHE ON ME

Breathe on me, breath of God,
fill me with life anew.
That I may love what Thou dost love,
and do what thou wouldst do.

Holy Spirit, breathe on me,
my stubborn will subdue.
Teach me in words of living flame,
what Christ would have me do.

Breathe on me, breathe on me; Holy Spirit.
The Celebration Hymnal

1 Peter 4:12-13 "Let not your heart be troubled:
ye believe in God, believe in me."

IN HIS CARE

In Christ we place our care,
as we look to the tomorrows.
In him it is a bonded affair,
for his grace we look afar.

Giving us courage for each step we take,
it is the knowing that instills hope.
A promise fulfilled, he did make,
a life line we can take.

So whatever transpires,
we are in his hands.
Such truth does inspire,
as we venture through his land.

Thought we do not see the future,
he has a wonderful plan.
His spirit to us does nurture,
it prepares us for a new home..

Say yes to his offer,
for we'll be in his care.
It is a promise for us all,
for it is Christ who calls.
It is he who beckons us in his care.

RG

"Christ liveth in me;....by the faith of
of the Son of God, who loved me and
gave Himself for me." (Gal. 2:17)

MEANINGLESS FAITH

For some people faith is a concept that is sometimes difficult to comprehend and narrow it down to a conclusive definition,. The reason is that it stems from the diversity of philosophies practiced and believed by so many people around the world. People go to church and claim they have the faith. The steeple, the pews or the stained glass windows are their Spirit. They serve as reminders that there is a Most High Priest and his name is Jesus Christ. The church is not the spirit. People read countless Christian books and say they are faithful. Is it the words of other people that convinced them that they have the faith? Some say they have faith because they associate with other Christians; go to Bible study and do a lot work for the church. Some say they responded to an alter call. Some people rely on the sinners prayer. A prayer that is worthless unless it is sincere and genuine commitment from the heart with a heart to heart abiding in the name and spirit of Jesus Christ. Some people say a few pious words in the presence of a minister. But was it said with conviction? Some say that they donate large sums of money and, therefore, claim to be in the faith and in good standings with Christ. Some say the Lord's Prayer, yet they don't recognize their own sins. All this is meaningless and worthless unless you followed Christ instructions. "It Is Wasted Faith." Paul tells us in II Corinthians what the prerequisites are for a genuine faith. "Examine yourselves, whether ye be in the faith; prove your own selves, have that Christ is in you, except ye be reprobates." Otherwise we are relying on the repetitious mouthing of words. Perhaps gambling our eternity.

The Spirit of Christ is integral to building a proper faith. One of the misconceptions people make is that they rely on their own sense of spiritual power. The profound reality is that we do not control our salvation. Such thinking leads us astray and can lead us down the wrong road. A road of dead-end streets. We wander aimlessly and become frustrated and confused. A road that doesn't guide us to salvation with Christ as the author. We must come face to face with the fact that faith is a gift built by the tutelage of our Lord. "A man can receive nothing, except it be given him from heaven." (John 3:27 KJ) "No man can come to me, except the Father which hath sent me and I will raise him up at the last day!" Salvation begins in the mind of God and is finished by Jesus Christ, our Lord. We don't have the authority to manipulate that power. Otherwise it is wasted faith. "See God's Whispering Hope." "But as many as received him, to them He gave the "right" to become children of God....(John 1:12-13 KJ) nor of the will of the flesh, nor the will of man, but of God." It is essential to grasp the belief that faith essentially starts with God. For without Jesus their wouldn't be an need for faith. It starts with him and is perpetuated by the spirit of our Lord working through us. Paul said "He made us alive together with Christ by his benevolent grace and unconditional love. Salvation is the most intimate relationship and covenant we can have through the Son of God. Actually, our future depends on it. Otherwise, it is wasted faith.

Christians are not a self-declared brother/sisterhood. It is an endorsed arrangement between two entities. Christ and another person. For faith depends on another person, that being our Lord and Savior. Memorizing scripture or going to church every Sunday does not in and of itself consummate a deal with Christ. Paul reminds us that "For to me to live in Christ, and to die is gain." The spirit must infuse and permeate our motivation for wanting to live in Christ. It is a calling by him, for him and through him. We, therefore, become the benefactor of his salvation. If we don't believe that, then we have wasted our faith and we'll be greatly disappointed when Jesus opens the door to heaven. Our hopes will be dashed on the rocks. Our spirit will live in darkness. Our heart will be broken. We will not see our Christian loved one again. For Christianity is living in the unity of the spirit which ultimately will be tested when we say good-bye to our family and friends on earth. The curious question is "Do you have faith in the person or your plan of salvation. It is the redemptive power and grace of our Lord that will satisfy our ultimate cry. It is by his grace that we become a child of God. He is the one who will give the certificate of reward for our faith. We hope that many people will not have to hear his voice say "I never knew you, depart from me, you who practice lawlessness." Many will let the love of God carry them in their faith. However, there will be many who are abandoned. Don't let your faith be wasted.

LORD, HEAR MY PRAYERS

THE LORD'S PRAYER

Our Father, who art in heaven, hallowed be Thy name. Thy Kingdom come, Thy will be done on earth as it is in heaven. Give us this day our daily bread, and forgive our debts as we forgive our debtors. And lead us not into temptaion, but deliver us from evil. For Thine is the kingdom and the power and glory. Amen

CHAPTER 8:

LORD HEAR MY PRAYERS

THE LORDS PRAYER

Our father who art in heaven, hallowed be Thy name. Thy Kingdom come, Thy will be done on earth as it is in heaven. Give us this day our daily bread, and forgive our debts as we forgive our debtors. And lead us not into temptation, but deliver us from evil. For Thine is the kingdom and the power and the glory. Amen

CHAPTER 8: LORD, HEAR MY PRAYERS

"And we know he hears us, we know that we have the petition that we desired of him." (1 John 5:15,KJ)

P =   You hear our "PETITIONS",
       especially our confessions.
       Whether big or small,
       we submit our calls.
       For you are our refuge,
       your benevolence is huge.

R =   On you is our "RELIANCE",
       faith must be in compliance.
       You are not far away,
       in our hearts each day.
       A spirit that transcends.
       on your faithfulness we depend.
       For our spirit to you ascends.

A =   To this we say "AMEN",
       when you bless women and men.
       Often your answers we don't hear,
       for your voice isn't clear.
       In your lofty heaven you reside,
       Oh, to hear your voice inward abide.

Y =   Often we peer "YONDER",
       to those miracles we wonder.
       When in solitude we utter prayers,
       knowing that you really care.
       Sometimes we think, are things really fair ?
       Then we remember, you know our prayers.

E = "ETERNALLY', though we pray today,
     sometimes we know that we'll hear you each day.
     Oh, the comfort of that reminisce,
     to Christianity that is the essence.
     For without you, troubles we could not dismiss,
     prayer neglected, surely our remiss.

R = Prayer, part of the "REVELATION",
     that our Lord holds us a special possession.
     His ears in tune to our hearts,
     never letting us drift apart
     For it is prayer that draws us together,
     during good times and bad weather.   RG

DOES GOD REALLY CARE?

The Bible tells of the good shepherd,
and that we are His flock.
For all humanity is a herd,
I will find you despite the size of the flock.

He knows our name and our pain,
when we have reason to complain.
He knows our face,
our identity He can trace.

He knows every born child,
on that thought dwell awhile.
I have written your name,
and will be with you in your land.
When to me you call,
I'll find you on the roll call.

Express your needs to me,
for I'll be with thee.
In me place your trust,
as through life you thrust.

In the mean- time you must smile,
for I'll be along in a little while.

RG

PRAYER

"Pray without ceasing." (1 Thess. 5:17,KJ)

Prayer is a means of communication with our Lord through the Holy Spirit. Like communion, we come into His presence, even though His presence surrounds us. We dial His number, O Lord, Jesus Christ, and he will listen to our supplications. The scriptures reveals the secret. "....when thou prayest, enter into they closet, and when thou hast shut the door, pray to thy Father which is in secret and thy Father which seeth in secret shall reward thee openly." (Matt 6:6, KJ) "For the eyes of the Lord are on the righteous. And His ears are open to their prayers." (1 Pet. 3:12,KJ) "Cast all your care upon Him; for He careth for you." (1 Pet. 5:7,KJ) "Come to Me, all you who labor and are heavy laden, and I will give you rest." (Matt. 11:28,KJ) Col. 9:12 " Phil. 4:5 "....but in every thing by prayer and supplication with thanksgiving let your requests be made known unto God." (Phil. 4:6,KJ) "give ear to my supplications: in thy faithfulness answer me." (Psalm 143:1,KJ) Amen.

Prayer can be broken down into categories depending on the nature of circumstances. For convenience only two will be mentioned.

A. Formal prayer: This is usually a more ritualistic approach as part of church liturgy such as a Sunday service   from prayer books, including weddings, or other special occasions. That is the reason why prayer is an integral part of the Christian Church. It is a more serious and fervent prayer submission to the Lord. Holy enough to require more reverence in the presence of God.

B General or daily prayer: Some people pray to the Lord to start the day, before each meal or at night before retiring for nightly rest. If we are cognizant of the encompassing Spirit of Christ, then sometimes intuitively or spontaneously we say "Thank You Lord !" as we walk or work through our daily responsibilities. This is particularly true when we encounter something beautiful such as spring flowers, a new born baby, a friend or a marriage bond to wife/husband. Regardless, God is is always there to listen. At least He promised that He would. Included within this grouping are prayers of praise. See below.

1. Intervention prayer: If a person is so inclined, your needs can be conveyed to priest or minister of your faith. In turn, they will present your wishes to the Lord. However, this doesn't circumvent personal responsibility.

2. Supplications: A plea for help. A grief to bear. A petition for God's intervention. Help, I am sad. I am unhealthy, I am dying or I am lonely, I need somebody with whom to talk.

Many times we take answered prayer for granted, thus we don't recognize when they have been fulfilled. They appear, it seems, automatically; such as our birth, our youth, marriage, our children, our education, our health, our job, God's provisions, etc. Everything all encompassing. Praying through extremely difficult times test our mind, body and soul, especially our spiritual stamina.

Hymn: Rev. 4:11. Thou Art Worthy
"You are worthy,
O Lord, To receive glory and honor and power;
For You created all things,
And by Your Will they exist and were created".

Hymn: Praise God From Whom All Blessings Flow.
Praise God from all blessings flow.
Praise Him, all creatures here below.
Praise Him above, ye heavenly Host.
Praise Father, Son and Holy Ghost.

Hymn: Acts 3:1 Sweet Hour Of Prayer.
Sweet hour of prayer, sweet hour of prayer.
That calls me from a world of care,
And bids me at my Father's throne,
Make all my wants and wishes known;

In season of distress and grief,
my soul has often found relief,
And oft escaped the tempter's snare,
by Thy return, sweet hour of prayer.

The wings shall my petition bear,
to Him whose truth and faithfulness,
engage the waiting soul to bless,
And since He bids me seek His face,
believe His Word, and trust His grace.
I'll cast on Him my every care,
and wait for thee, sweet hour of prayer.

Psalm 111: Praise the Lord !

I will praise the Lord with my heart,
in the assembly of the upright and in the congregation,
the works of the Lord are great.
Studied by all who have pleasure in them.
His work is honorable and glorious,
and His righteousness endures forever.
He has made His wonderful works to be remembered.

The theme of this book gives credit as a form of remembrance for the gifts God has given to me. Most of which relates to God's creative genius and His saving grace. Much of these things are beyond description and comprehension. Therefore, it behooves us to bow our heads and say "Thank You, Lord!"

ALL THINGS FROM HEAVEN

All things from God descended,
on which we have depended.

Houses, cars, tables and chairs,
materials provided by a God who cares.

Many harbor this with greed,
rather than share the seed.

God says, don't take this for granted !
For you may end up empty handed.

Be grateful and say "Thank You Lord !".
It is I who gave you the gifts twofold,
In your hands and heart to hold.

An earth on which to survive,
sustaining life until to me you arrive.

Though I ask you to run a race,
in faith hold a steady pace.
For My Son has told you the reason why,
for tomorrow will apply

All creation to enjoy,
to us God did deploy.
So many are these treasures,
to satisfy our pleasures,
Say, "Thank You Lord !"

Parents who gave us birth,
Their hearts filled with mirth,
coached us through the years.
Sometimes with tears,
oft times to calm the fears.

Always there with loving care,
say, "Thank You Lord!"

A loving wife, marriage recited,
hand and hand united.
A mate throughout life,
together coping with strife.
Facing all the tomorrows, many a dream to follow.
Then to them is born a child(s),
they lived with us for awhile.

Raised and then departed,
loving memories fill the sweet hearted.

Say, "Thank You Lord !"

RG

"....for your heavenly Father knoweth that ye have need of all these things." (Mat. 6:32,KJ)

"The Lord is close to everyone who prays to Him, To all who truly pray to Him." (Psalm 145:18,IBML)

"I have called upon you, for you will hear me, O God; incline your ear to me, and hear my speech." (Psalm 17"6,IBML)

"....know how to give good gifts unto your children, how much more shall your Father which is in heaven give good things to them that ask him?" (Matt. 7:11,KJ)

"Praying always with all prayer supplications in the Spirit." (Ehp. 6:18, KJ)

"Likewise the Spirit also helps in our weaknesses, for we do not know what we should pray for as we ought.: (Rom. 8:26,IBML)

"And you will call upon me and find me, when you search for me with all your heart." (Jer. 29:11.IBML)

"For through Him we both have access to the Father by one spirit. And he who searches our hearts knows the mind of the Spirit." (Eph. 2:18, BBML)

GOD'S GIFT SHOPPE

How often we've heard,
God is our refuge.
Take it in prayer to the Lord,
in the hymnal that's the message.

Like sheep He is our shepherd,
He'll answer our prayers.
Often we do this in error,
using God like a gift shopper.

God neglected day after day,
then we dare send requests His way.
How selfish are these displays,
He rejects such inequities.

How foolish such irreverence.
A dilemma in the time of need,
then we cry out and plead.
In crisis or peril or tragedy,
we then acknowledge His deity.

How false this infirmity,
a habit lacking responsibility.
Certainly not God's expectation,
this exploitation.

Through prayer God is our line of communication,
fellowship is the intention.
To worship a divine source,
for God is our resource.

Faith is a spiritual activity,
an act done in soliloquy.
In our hearts to fill this obligation,
a Christian with devotion.

Your petitions submit in sincerity,
but sent with humility.
Prayer is our soul reaching to extend,
beyond self it transcends.

A privilege our prayers to send,
on God we can depend.
Our heart filled with need,
our soul He'll lead.

Fate shakes the foundation of our destiny,
distraught with grief and anxiety.
God says, come to me,
I will comfort thee.
A Christian you must be,
through Christ is our destiny.

RG

BLESSINGS COME OUR WAY

I awake each morning, God's blessings to view,
they come as a generous flow.
To my senses they ensue,
in our hearts it is quite a show.

You designed an earth enshrined,
Your glorious display is our clue.
For you have been generous and kind,
We learn this when setting in pew.
Your grace does feed our soul,
it feeds our spirit and make it new.

Even the animals, birds and flowers,
extend a "Thank you" your way.
For you are with us each day,
without you these blessings would not stay.

You bathe us with your spirit,
washing away our sorrows.
Giving us strength, if we admit,
helping us to face all the tomorrows.

In these things we delight,
for they bring us pleasures.
Truly a magnificent sight,
we applaud your treasures.

Blessings that come our way,
each and every day.

RG

"....for you heavenly Father knoweth that
we have need of all these things." (Matt.6:32)

THE RESTLESS SEA

The sea, the restless sea,
like life, its turbulence we can't flee.
On the rocks dreams are dashed,
some times in endless waves.
They burst onto the shore splashed.
Yet, their fulfillment the soul craves.

But wait, look to the horizon,
waves appear by the dozens.
Some destroy, others are good,
God tells us this should be understood.
Some are blessings, while from others we learn,
that counting our blessings carries us over the churn.
Shaping our faith, knowing God is in control.
Hang on to this as through life you stroll.

The sea gull flies above the turbulence,
wings spread and carried by the wind.
Reminding us of God's plan and His benevolence.
Keep forging those dreams and listen to the
"Whispering hope" of the wind.

The clouds above, though they dim our view,
see the sun, the Son "Christ" shines on the sea.
This is true !

With love,
Dad, August 2003

HYMN: THANKS BE TO GOD

Thanks to God for my redeemer,
Thanks for all Thou dost provide!
Thanks for times now but a memory,
Thanks for Jesus by my side,
Thanks for pleasant, balmy spring time,
Thanks for dark and stormy fall!
Thanks for tears by now forgotten,
Thanks for peace within my soul!

Thanks for prayers that thou hast answered,
Thanks for what Thou dost deny!
Thanks for storms that I have weathered,
Thanks for all Thou dost supply!
Thanks for pain, and thanks for pleasure,
Thanks for grace that none can compare!

Thanks for roses by the wayside,
Thanks for thorns and thanks for fireside,
Thanks for hope, the sweet refrain!
Thanks for joy and thanks for sorrow,
Thanks for heavenly peace with Thee,
Thanks through all eternity!

"Words: R.T.Brooks
C 1954, Ren. 1982 Hope Publishing Co.
Carol Stream, IL 60188. All rights reserved.
Used by permission. Reprinted under license #65475"

GOD'S LOVE STORY

CHAPTER 9:

APPROACHING SALVATION

"If thou shalt confess with they mouth the Lord Jesus,
and shalt believe in thine heart that God hath raised
him from the dead, thou shalt be saved." (Rom. 10:9)

It should be held paramount as to how the practice of salvation impacts a person mentally, emotionally and spiritually. Post salvation can in some cases be more disastrous than before the event. Especially when it comes to improper preparation of a person prior to approaching Jesus for his gift of redemption. This is further compounded and complicated when there is inadequate or no follow-up after making the commitment at the alter. Christian psychologist reveals numerous such cases. Promises made, but not fulfilled. This in particular pertains to large mass revival meetings. The service is closed by giving the invitation to an alter call. I presume that it is more a case of mass hypnosis or mental suggestion that influences people to respond, rather than the indwelling Holy Spirit. Especially young people who put their trust in influential leaders. A close look at Christ's redeeming power is not only essential, but is paramount to salvation and understanding. Total awareness must precede such a sanctified gift from our Lord. For He is the author and the giver of a forgiving grace.

At so many rival meetings or Church services a few choice scripture readings and a few choice hymns such as "Jesus Loves Me" and "Just as I am" are sung. We must be cognizant of the fact that there is a condition called mass hypnosis. A situation where the commitment is more a psychological reason rather than a conviction of the heart, mind and soul. Hymns that play on the emotions of a person rather than a more thorough methodology to properly prepare a person to develop a genuine frame of mind to approach his/her Lord and Savior. Then there is the approach where a Pastor says " Come to my office and I'll get you saved". A fifteen minute conference in a Pastor's office is not sufficient time to explore the parameters of this Holy experience and gift. The Pastor says "You're troubles will be taken away by Jesus and you'll find peace". Then the person is left to cope with the balance between the realities of life and spirituality. Then there is the fear approach "You'll live for eternity in hell" or " Jesus might come tomorrow". This I shall call alarmism or defeatism. An approach that degrades a persons self esteem. Pastor's do not know the integrity and self-esteem of a person setting in their congregation. Then, of course, there is pressure from the Pastor, parents and friends. Of course none of these reasons are worthy enough for any person to approach our Lord for his grace and redemption. Pastor's must be more thoroughly aware of the degree to which they influence the minds of people . There are diverse reasons for a person to respond to an alter call. But, have they chosen the right reason and purpose ? Furthermore, we must realize that Jesus is not seen in person today. We can not see his eyes as he looks into ours and express his caring and loving grace toward us. We can't touch his robe or feel the touch of his hands. Nor do we hear his voice with the significance of his words "You are forgiven and you are now a son of God through me." We cope with the invisible spirit today. That is a tremendous barrier and ordeal for many people today. They battle with a Holy Ghost, one that many ministers should translate more effectively and consciously.

I can say this with confidence, because at the age of seventeen I fell victim to an evangelical preacher. He told the congregation, mostly teenagers, that if we are saved Jesus will come down and walk with you. Teenagers are especially wide open to such speculation. Based on that promise I approached the alter. After experiencing that moment I did not hear, touch or see Jesus. An experience that had significant ramifications for the next forty-five years of my life. I took on the attitude and belief that Christ had rejected me and spiritually I lived accordingly. As a teacher I had a student who rushed into my office filled with excitement, Mr. Goodman " I was saved last night at a revival gathering". I replied "Congratulations !". Then he hurried off to his first morning class. When I arrived at school the next morning, I was informed that he had gone home after school and committed suicide with the Bible on his chest and a plastic bag over bis head. What a shame and tragedy. In my readings I have learned that the aftermath of salvation can lead to very disturbing problems for a variety of spiritual reasons. To whom should the finger of blame be pointed ? Because of God's instructions we are all responsible. There should be a more serious attempt to orient and prepare young people minds and spirit in preparation for one of the most important events and celebrations in their lives. It is a matter of shedding light on God's greatness. It is also an indication of God's work in His son's and daughter's. For through Christ we inherit the title "God's Children" and we are all brothers and sisters united in the spirit of our Lord.

Not to provide better orientation to salvation is a disservice to our Lord, Jesus Christ. Perhaps it breaches the intent of Christ's voluntary act on the cross. The Pastor does not possess the power to bring about the redemption of a single soul, nor does baptism. For salvation is a covenant between the confirmation of a persons heart and Jesus Christ, our Lord and Savior. The minister provides the setting and guides as prescribed by God's Holy Word. Many people get hung up on this issue. Pastors can not and should not control the works of the Holy Spirit. The spirit of Christ is free roaming to whom ever wishes to receive it. Perhaps some ministers should be more cautious and give consideration to what Jesus wants us to do. He is the boss.

Understanding should precede salvation in order to fathom God's expectations of us. If a prospective candidate for salvation is not aware of inherent factors, then he/she approaches Jesus grace in blind faith. The approach should be genuine for Jesus to receive us. The result will be that the person will grope with the struggles of faith, rather than discover the fruits of knowing and having a positive relationship with Christ. In the end it renders a person, to some degree, helpless in coping with the interrelationship of realities of life and the Father, Son and Holy Ghost. The relationship becomes a sense of "Where are you Lord ?". It is important to comprehend the workings of the Holy Spirit before approaching our Lord in a heart to heart affair. More so, it is a faith to faith spiritual encounter or marriage united in one spirit. Unless this is fully understood, Christ's grace and mercy can become a muddled affair. An improper and inadequate approach can and will foster a spiritually detrimental experience. Thus, resulting in a weakened faith plagued by continual lack of confidence and trust in the Holy One who wants to deliver us from agonies bondage. Too many ministers lose sight of this aspect of Christianity and the responsibilities inherent to being Christ's messenger. It compromises the fullness of the definition and purpose of infusing God's Will as it applies to humanity. This is not to pass judgment, but to focus on the concerns associated with the practice of salvation. In other words, how it is interwoven into the fabric of Christian philosophy.

We need to be more conscience of how to instill the Holy Spirit and prevent spiritual harm, but to release the love of God in our lives. Letting God do His work in each individual life. For we are His helper and witness the power of the spirit that drives us forward, not only in our faith, but our works as well. Works are important for it reveals the special gift born to each of us. Approaching salvation and our works are an integral part of "The Wonder of it all". God did not make us robots, he programmed each of us for a reason. Whether it be for the world or for Him. God is a God of variety and the people of this world represent a composite mix of abilities and ambitions.

I have difficulty listening to a sermon in a Sunday morning church service and hear the repetitious syndrome of sinner ! Sinner ! Sinner! It certainly doesn't ring a positive note in the hearts of the listeners. Yes, by the acts of Adam and Eve we inherited the sins of human kind. However, such a metronome of a word degrades a person, their esteem and dignity. All of which were gifted to each of us by God himself. That is what makes up our character and personality. It promotes a sense of defeatism, frustration and confusion as we venture into the next week. I don't recall Christ saying to his congregations sinner ! Sinner ! Sinner ! His approach was love and grace. Sometimes I think the only word ministers learned in seminary school is the pronunciation and definition of the word sinner. God did not say, destroy the sinner but to encourage people into His Kingdom. For we are His children, not under the ownership of a Pastor or, for that matter, any of us. Let God do His work freely and unobstructed. In architectural design and building we do not tear down the frame work of a bridge or multilevel structure to finish it. Edification is necessary to reveal the beauty and purpose of the spirit of each individual person. Each human being is edified according God's wishes to function as an individual in the Christian community. Though we are different, God has a purpose for each of us. To forcefully try to bend a person into a spiritual shape prescribed by another person is against Gods Will. Each of us, regardless of our heritage, is part of God's Master Plan.

One of the primary reasons for writing this book "The Wonder of it all" is directly linked to what has been afore said. I want to help young people, non-believers and atheists to avoid the stumbling blocks to which I have been subjected in my religious walk. Hopefully, it will fill in some of the holes to their approach to salvation. Salvation is planting a seed and watch it grow like a flower. Don't' hinder its growth by condemnation. Nourish it and encourage its growth. The result will be wonderful in the eyes of Christ and the beholder. There must be a preparedness before entering the sanctuary with Jesus Christ. The approach must be genuine. Remember, we must rely on "God Whispering Hope". Exploring "The Wonder of it All" serves as a foundation of dwelling with God's creative genius and Christ's redemptive grace, "...with the comfort with which we ourselves are comforted by God." (2 Cor.l :4,IBML) Exploration of Gods mysteries has brought a degree of comfort and peace to my life. It helps identify who we are in God's Kingdom. The fact that we are a child when hugged by the spirit of Jesus makes us joint heirs in "The Wonder of it all". We are joined together and united in the affairs of Jesus. His spirit working through us perpetuates our words, our works, our desires, our dreams and our expectations to please him. It demonstrates the Holy Spirit at work in our lives.

If we pay attention as we traverse through God's spiritual kingdom and study His creative genius as well as His grace through salvation our lives take on a new dimension. Our eyes see visions that shape our minds, our attitudes as well as our hearts. With our ears tuned in we hear the Holy spirit speaking to us through "The Wonder of it all". We see the presence of God every where and see the amazing power of His works in the lives of other people. Revelations 4:11

"You are worthy, O Lord, to receive glory and honor and peace; for you created all things, and by your will they exist and were created." (Rev. 4:11, IBML) Every praise that erupts from our senses goes to the designer of "The Wonder of it all". We exist because God exists. We live because God granted us the gift of life. We shall have eternal life because of His Son who paid the price on the cross. His remarkable love and grace is beyond measure. "How shall we escape, if we neglect so great salvation." (Heb. 2:3KJ) It is ours for the asking accompanied by a genuine reason. I'll do it because other people are doing it is not a good or righteous reason. Christ will know the difference. If it is not done in earnest and with a pure heart he will ignore you. There is more than forgiveness at stake, there is also integrity and honesty at stake. If we expect him to cleanse us completely without one stain then we must believe in that promise. For it sets the stage for eternity. It is a free gift granted by the most High Priest. To some degree it is not free. For we must be transformed in our minds, heart and soul. Christ sacrificed his body for us, therefore, we must also sacrifice to live in his image. 2 Corinthians 4:4 "....Christ, now is the image of God, should shine unto them." (2 Cor. 4:4,KJ) " "Looking to Jesus the author and finisher of our faith." (Heb. 12:2, KJ)

Studying "The Wonder of it all" instills in us a great sense of hope. To engage in the discipline of discovering God through such wonders requires patience. Learning is a process of educational building blocks. This is also true of faith and hope. Faith does not occur at the snap of a finger. It is not spontaneous like an injection of medication. This is probably one of the biggest pit falls that traps our emotions and understanding. It takes time to grow in the faith, whether it be in a general sense or in Jesus Christ. Of course, many times it is our own fault. However, ministers should be fully aware of how to properly prepare a person before approaching salvation. This is based on my personal experience and observations.

"....be transformed by the renewal of your mind, that you may prove what is the will of God, what is good and acceptable and perfect." (Rom. 12:1,2, KJ) This is an important aspect of salvation. For through salvation we take on the image of Christ to the best of our knowledge and ability. Out of "The Wonder of it all" comes the wonders of Gods love and grace. Through our visionary senses we can imagine the power of His might and the ever presence of His spirit through us. For we are His workmanship. The spirit is an infusion of His Will. Where we willfully guide our lives and relationships according to His expectations of us. We do not become puppets to accomplish this holy assignment, but in partnership. A covenant beyond explanation. An agreement we can't afford to ignore. A Holy spiritual contract signed and sealed with the love of our Lord. Hebrews 13:5 " ....he said, I will never leave thee or forsake you." (Heb. 13:5, KJ) The stamp of approval is Christ hanging on the tree. How many people listen to the Pastor rather than the echo of their own hearts ? The Pastor doesn't own the Holy Spirit. It roams as free as the wind. It stirs our minds, our conscience and our hearts. It plucks the heart strings of every supposedly saved Christian. So the questions arises "Do we listen to the Pastor as the last word or do we embrace and respond to the hymn sung in our hearts. Is it Christ who is calling where we are in tune with His Spirit.

What is salvation ?
It's two hearts tied together in
"The Spirit of Christ"

THE POWER OF THE SPIRIT

Oh, the power of imagination.

Oh, the power of inspiration.

Oh, the power of God's grace.

Oh, the power of vision.

Oh, the power of bathing in the spirit.

Oh, the power of Christ's redemption.

Oh, the power of encouragement.

Oh, the power of residing in the presence of the Lord.

Oh, the power of God's creative genius.

Oh, the power of His abundance.

Oh, the strength of His blessings.

Oh, the power of placing our care in the hands of the good Shepard.

Oh, the power of genuine faith in Christ's promises.

Oh, the hope of a new dawning.

Oh, the power of His silent voice.

Oh, the power of victory over death.

Oh, the power of "The Wonder of it all" wrought by the
Master's Hands.
RG

FORGIVENESS

F = "Forbearance" in the wake of sin,
     when patience grows thin.
     "Forgiveness" an act of grace,
     taught by Christ, the origin if we trace.

O = Sin, where is its "Origin",
     mans deeds which trespass, there it begins.

R = Our failure to be "Reverent."
     such things God does resent.

G = They cause our "Grieving",
     Christ said, "Forgive seventy times seven."

I = This instruction we should "Internalize",
     obedience to Gods Word, in life to realize.

V = Into forgiveness each day we "Venture",
     it dwells with us as we face the future.

E = It effects our "Eternity",
     our relations with the Holy Trinity.

N = The grace of forgiveness Christ teaches us to "Nurture."
     His mercy He gives free and true.

E = A gift "Everlasting",
     there for the asking.

S = It requires admission and confession of "Sins."
     Reborn and a new life to begin.

S = Honor, worship and praise His Holy "Sovereignty."
     God's Will tells of its certainty.

                                              RG

The Lord said, "Forgive those who trespass against us, and forgive our trespasses"

It is one of the ingredients to the "Bread of Life."

Why did God include forgiveness ? It is an act of grace to mend the heart strings so that all hearts beat in unison for the purpose of harmony for the good of all.

Note: The poem is not intended to be a mockery of "Forgiveness." Christ tells us that it is a serious matter. He should know, he demonstrated it on the cross.

"....being justified by His grace through the redemption that is in Christ Jesus. Whom God sent forth as a propitiation by His blood, through faith, to demonstrate His righteousness, because in His forbearance God had passed over the sins that were previously committed, to demonstrate at the present time His righteousness, that He might be just and the justifier of the one who has faith in Jesus." (Rom.3:24m IBML)

"Therefore, He also is able to the uttermost those who come to God through Him, since He always live to make intercession for them." (Heb. 7:25,JJ3ML)

Interpretation: This specifically states that Jesus Christ has the authority and redemptive power to be our advocate to present us to God, his Father, our creator, and His love story grant us permission to dwell with Him for eternity. This means that He will try his uttermost to represent us favorable in the sight of God. the Holy One and the most High. The prerequisite, as declared by God, is our salvation (reborn, saved) and cleansed by baptism to be made presentable before the throne of God. In this is eternal truth and hope through our faith and trust of God's promises.

Scripture: Christ said "It is finished!" He paid the price for our inequities. "I will not cast you out." "Who His own self bore our sins in His own body on the tree." (1 Pet. 2:24,KJ)

HYMN: BE THOU MY VISION

Be Thou my vision,
0 Lord of my heart;
Naught be all else to me,
save that Thou art.

Thou my best thought,
by day and by night.
Waking or sleeping,
Thy presence my light.

Be Thou my wisdom and,
Thou my true word;
I ever with Thee and,
Thou with me Lord:

Thou my great Father,
I Thy true son.
Thou in me dwelling,
and I with Thee one.

Riches I heard not,
nor man's empty praise.
Thou mine inheritance,
now and always;

Thou and Thou only,
first in my heart.
High King of heaven,
my treasure Thou art.

High King of heaven,
my victory own.
May I reach heavens joys,
bright heaven's sun !

Heart of my own heart,
whatever befall.
Still be my vision,
O Ruler of all.

The Celebration Hymnal

Wow! Wow! Wow!
What expectations to reach
the Bible does teach.
This is why we fall short of God.
Yet, we try as through life we trod.
If it were not for Christ's forgiveness,
we should be in a heck of a mess.
Praise God for His everlasting grace !

HIS GRACIOUS WONDERS

Yes, we are God's field. It is His wish and desire to plant seeds of wisdom in our conscience. He then watches as we grow and mature in the Spirit of Christ. He cultivates us, nurtures us and encourages us to grow as best as we can in faith. In other words, reap the harvest. Then our spirit is free to worship and praise His works in us. As a direct result we are given the fruit to feed other people. Feed ourselves, the nation and the world. We bear fruit not only to please Him, but for our spirituality as well. The Holy Spirit fertilizes our very being, Jesus said "That I will pour out of my Spirit on all flesh (us)." It is like the wind or radio frequences that touch all humanity. The earth as well as us are God's garden. He is constantly planting His seeds in the hearts of those who will receive it.

If you have a hymnal, in particular The Celebration Hymnal, please turn to "The Wonder Of It All." Now read all the verses and draw your own conclusions. Then to the best of your ability determine the significance of the message it delivers as it applies to your spiritual well being. It not only recognizes God's creative genius, but His gracious love toward us, His children. It clearly depicts that He is showering down on us His love to help us through life on a daily basis. Even to the point that we should hang on and trust Him until from this earth we depart. He is with us even until the end time. We become the recipients of His love and grace. Oh, the power of His Spirit. A scripture reading that further influences these words is Heb. 2:6 KJ "What is a human being that you care for him?" Eph. 2:4 KJ "But God, who is rich in mercy, for His great love wherewith He loved us." "And both raised us up together and made us sit in a heavenly place in Christ Jesus." John 4:10 KJ "If thou knowest the gift of God, and who it is that saith to thee, give me to drink; thou wouldest have asked him, and he would have given thee living waters." The water is God's spirit and love poured out to us.

LOVE OF GOD

L =   "Lord" His mercy and grace toward us,
        For His children he makes a fuss.
        Love that exceeds ours,
        There each living hour.

O =   His "Oath" until the end time,
        We give thanks, for it is thine.
        He says it is true,
        To give life anew.

V =   "Voluntary" on the cross,
        On him he bore the yoke,
        Forgives, mercy, love; evil he crushed.
        Of this the disciples spoke.

E =   "Everlasting" is his grace,
        A promise that gives our steps an assured pace.
        Thank you for your love,
        All coming from above.

                            RG

CROSSING LIFE'S BRIDGES

Through life we walk,
crossing many bridges.
Of this journey, I now talk.
The genetic code of life,
passed through the ages.
Then we turn the pages,
now let us recall the stages.

First we are born,
then through infancy we struggle.
Without parents we would be forlorn,
they bestow their love with a cuddle.

Then we encounter youth and the teenage years,
many time experiencing fears.
Our parents' love dried the tears,
helping us to the future peer.

Then on to adulthood,
with the responsibilities of manhood.
And woman with motherhood,
with Christ teaching us to live in brotherhood.

The final bridge to cross is from life to the eternal realm,
with Christ Jesus at the helm.
But wait, there is another bridge to cross,
before we reach the cross.
We must cross the bridge of salvation,
there is no other conclusion.

For it is our transgressions,
when forgiven by Christ it gives new direction.
Salvation is a special bridge to cross,
Christ gave it to us on the cross.
Redemption for our soul to cleanse,
like the purity of a crystal lens.

Birth....to youth....to adulthood we all must pass.
Salvation...to Christian brotherhood...to Christ's care
we pass.
Before we can reach the cross, without alas !
Christ helps us to cross the bridge to God's eternal plan
each day.
May God bestow His blessings on us each day.

The bridges of our life,
rest in God's Grace !
Through Him we are given new life,
then God we can embrace.

RG

DISCOVERING OUR NEEDS

Matt: 6:32 "Your heavenly Father knows all your needs."

Why write poetry, stories, prayers, or design and fabricate stained glass work? It provides the opportunity to fortify our mental as well as our spiritual well being. It is a form of therapy. It puts us in moments of quietude, where we can focus, reflect and concentrate on our selves and all that is in us. The Lord said "Examine yourselves". Furthermore, to be able to become cognizant of the blessings God has bestowed on us or what other people have done for us. It becomes a personal time to pull our thoughts together. Thereby, providing time to think, organize and foster ways to bring our affairs into a new perspective. Periodic modification is good for the soul. We become a better person; more joyous, more patient and more fruitful.

"But we believe that through the grace of the Lord, Jesus Christ, we shall be saved..." (Acts. 15:11, KJ)

"If you abide in me and my words abide in you, you will ask what you desire, and it shall done for you." (John 15:7, IBML)

"Trust in the Lord, and do good...And he shall give us the desires of your heart." (Psalm 37:3-6 JBML)

"And God is able to make all grace abound toward you; that ye, always having all sufficiency in all things, may abound to every good work." (2Cor. 9:8,KJ)

Psalm 118 "Oh, give thanks to the Lord, for He is good! Because his mercy endureth for ever.")Psalm 118, KJ) "that if thou shalt confess with they mouth the Lord Jesus, and shalt believe in thine heart that God hath raised him from the dead, thou shalt be saved." (Rom10:9-10,KJ)

"Ponder the path of thy feet, and let they ways be established." (Prov.4:25,KJ)

GOD'S BENEVOLENT LOVE

From our creator unceasing,
    I see it at work in you.

It comes to our heart unfailing,
    making His promises ever true.

It is a divine source,
    yet, through His Son he gave it free.

It guides us on our course,
    like the winds gentle breeze.

It strengthens our faith,
    if only in Him we trust.

Behold it keeps us on the path,
    to follow him is a must.

Believe and we are transformed,
    for his love is forever.

By him your faith is formed,
    a spirit that will dwell forever.

Through him and his grace,
    he clothes us to be immortal.

Heart to heart we embrace,
    As we invision heavens portal.
                      RG

"I am with you always, even unto the
    end of the world." (Matt. 28:20 KJ)

CHAPTER 10:

CHRIST JESUS REDEMPTIVE POWER

On the cross He bore our pain,
for us he was slain.
With a spear His blood was shed,
in our place He suffered instead.

A gift beyond compare to treasure,
for He gave His love in full measure.
Though we walk in our transgressions,
He honors our plea for His intercessions.

Giving us freedom and liberty,
to live unshackled to our inequity.
Free to walk in the grip of His grace,
to our spirit it strengthens the pace.
Giving us endurance to reinforce our faith,
as we sojourn along life's path.

His sacrifice is impossible to repay,
futile to think that way.
For it would question Christ's voluntary act,
it would be our shame to tarnish this fact.

We search for words of gratitude,
all He wants is a Christian attitude.
Oh Lord, thanks for your redemptive power.
Grant me the power to over earthly struggles tower.

Oh Lord, defend me before your Father.
To His Holy goodness make fast my tether.

RG

WHAT ABOUT THE GOSPEL?

We have heard it said "The Gospel Truth"
It was about Christ's mission.
Sent by his Father, to reveal that He cares,
it was a heartfelt decision.

It was reported by Mark, Luke and John,
to tell us of Christ's plan.
Often told by minister's sincere, who carry on
an old story conveyed as often as they can.

We love to hear it once again,
for it holds promises for future years.
A birth-right we can claim,
a Savior who takes away fears.

We march forward with steadfast belief,
it quickens our steps, step by step.
By our faith it gives relief,
a story that carries us over the hills, none are too steep.

It is a story of redemptive grace,
it helps us to finish the race.
A grace to have if we beleive in the gospels,
written for us as we Christians stroll.
Through life it is a divine spell.

For it is faith that justifies,
when we accept his sacrifice.
We must realize that story was written by the Son of God,
free for asking if we repent.

Some people along life plod,
others aware of Christ's special event.
That is why Christian's have an assignment,
As we travel through life's passage.

What about the gospel?
it is the truth told by Mark, Luke and John.

RG

"Looking to Jesus the author and
finisher of our faith." (Heb. 13:5)

LINES IN THE SAND

"How shall we escape, if we neglect so great salvation?"
(Heb. 2:3,KJ)

Most of us have heard or read the brief analogy of foot prints in the sand. A story that Christ carries us throughout our Christian life. That he is always there to help us to cope with the realities of life, in other words, our trials and tribulations that cause us pain, sorrow or grief. However, we must also face the unrelenting fact that God (Christ) purposely draws lines in the sand. Let us take a look at the lines he has drawn in the sand.

1. Life: God created the life "line" (genetics) for all of humanity. A life chuck full of wonderful things. God's creative genius on display.

2. Adam and Eve: The first born by the hands of God and provided a paradise for them to live in with all the necessary provisions to enjoy a happy life. However, Eve enticed Adam to commit a sin. God was greatly displeased, even to the point of drawing a "line" between himself and humankind. We, today, don't have any choice. For by inheritance we took on the same sinful nature. Why did God draw a "line" of demarcation between himself and his children? He had discovered that humankind was full of sinful things. God can not look on a sinful person. However, rather than being a controlling God where humankind became His robots, out of love for us, he granted us freedom. Freedom of will to live according to our selfish desires and satisfactions. Of course, we realize that path leads to destruction and without hope at the end of life on his temporal earthly dwelling place. In other words, simply put, life would be a dead end street. On the other hand, out of God's grace, he offers us a second choice. Which is a decision to walk in partnership with Him in our earthly life as well as into everlasting life. Scripture: John 14:3 "where I am, you may be also".

3. Dead end streets: We draw lines in the sand separating us from The Good Shepard.
   a. Don't honor, respect or worship our creator.
   b. Don't love or forgive your neighbor.
   c. Don't obey God's commandments.
   d. Don't live a grateful life.
   e. Don't be fruitful by not using your God given endowment of abilities (innate gifts),
   f. Don't repent of your sins.
   g. Don't approach Christ for salvation.
   h. Don't believe that Christ can issue you redemption through his benevolent grace. In other words, ignore or reject his salvation. That is precisely why he was born.God's Son, earth child, who came to witness and rescue us form our self inflected sinful ways.
   i. Attending church will not give a person salvation and eternal life. People can attend church all there lives and never be saved.
   j. We can read the Bible a thousand times and never be saved. Including the memorization of countless scriptural passages.
   k. We can donate large sums of money to the church & never enter God's Kingdom.
   l. We can volunteer to do Christian work many times over and still not be saved. A man without arms and legs can be saved by the grace of God.
   m. We can be good using our own measuring stick, but we are measured by God's Standards. One of our biggest fallacies.

"Never the less the foundation of God standeth sure, having this seal, the Lord knoweth them that are His." (2 Tim.2:19,KJ) ".....that where I am, there ye may be also." (John 14:3,KJ)

Notice: I am not implying that any of the above is not to be considered a significant part of living a Christian life. A Christian life is a blend of all these factors.

SO, WHAT IS THE SECRET?

4. The path of faith and salvation: Some people think that faith is not necessary for salvation or that faith will get us to heaven. Sadly, that is false thinking. For there is a direct linkage between the two dimensions of spirituality. It is faith, trust and hope in Jesus Christ's voluntary act on the tree that gives us not only the purpose, but also the reason, courage and conviction to approach Jesus Christ's image. Our faith must be sufficiently established before approaching the Most High Priest to avoid misconceptions about what transpires when Christ forgives our transgressions and offers his hand of acceptance into his Holy Spirit. Hebrews 11:6. "But without faith it is impossible to please Him". Ephesians 2:8. "For by grace are ye saved through faith". Romans 8:23 "....even we ourselves groan within ourselves waiting the adoption, the redemption of our body. For we are saved in this hope." (Rom.8:23,KJ) Note that this is preceded by our faith and the act of salvation. It is an adoption of unconditional love. Remember the hymn "Just as I am." I use the word unconditional loosely for there are conditions in our relationship of such a Holy magnitude. We must approach salvation discretely with honesty, integrity and sincerity of the heart. Otherwise, we fool ourselves and approach him with false intentions or, perhaps, with half-heartedness. God will not bale us out if we are not in a repentant mind set. The consequences can be emotionally and spiritually debilitating. Even experiencing confusion, frustration and a questioning mind full of doubts. There must be a genuine faith in the Son of God. It is through him that we become son's and daughter's of God everlasting. All part of the "Wonder of it all."

Now, Baptism vs. Salvation to enter God's Kingdom. There is a significant difference between the two birth rights. If we study Johns baptism of Jesus closely, not once did Jesus say "This is for the forgiveness of sins of humankind, nor did he say " This I do so that you will have eternal life". Jesus baptism was a public display to demonstrate the purity of himself in the eyes of his believers. Primarily for the purpose of assurance (authenticity) that he truly was the Son of God filled with his holiness. As a matter of fact, God shouted from the clouds "This is my Son and I am pleased with him." Thus declaring Jesus righteousness and rightful place in the Kingdom of God. Unfortunately, many people don't know the difference between the birth right of baptism and salvation by way of the cross. Thus generating a state of spiritual confusion. Salvation is by way of the cross and the redemption therein. Christ died on the cross to free us from the burden of our iniquities. Being forgiven of our transgressions we have a clean heart on which God can look and sanctify our faith, in adddition, Christ grants us permission and the privilege of "crossing a line in the sand". Jesus says "Cross over the line and follow me". After crossing the "line" of salvation Christ scribes a "line" in the sand to follow. The glory of God will crown you with a reward beyond your imagination. The culmination of a life long search of waiting as we discover "The Wonder of it all." Baptism vs. salvation? Personally, I am inclined to devote my faith to Jesus Christ as the mediator of my soul. Phil. 2:12 "Therefore, my dear friends continue to work out your salvation. Prove to the world that we are Christians. Because it is God working in you, both in the willing and the doing". Paul is reminding the Christians in Philippi to stay focused on Jesus Christ. The Lord's Prayer says" "....give us our daily bread". It causes us to rejoice with words, voice and deeds. The poems bear witness that a soul is working out his salvation through Christ's redemptive power. Each morning God awakes us and introduces us to the "Wonders of Salvation."

5. The path and the reasons why:

    a. "For God sent not his Son into the world to condemn the world; but that the world through him might be saved." (John 3:17JfCJ) It certainly was an indication of His optimism for humanity.

b. 2 Timothy 3:15. "....make thee wise unto salvation through faith which is in Christ Jesus." (2 Tim.3:15,KJ) Note: This is the linkage of salvation and faith.

c. " God is a shield unto them that put their trust in him." (Prov. 30:5.KJ)

d. "....there is one God, and one mediator between God and men, the man Christ Jesus." (1 Tim. 2:5,KJ)

e. " Jesus saith unto him, I am the way, the truth, and the life: no man cometh unto the Father, but by me." (John 14:6,KJ) Note: That is the way of the cross.

f. "....but the gift of God is eternal life through Jesus Christ our Lord." (Rom.6:23)

g. "....God hath given to us eternal life, and this life is in His Son." (1 John 5:11,KJ)

h. "....that believing ye might have life through his name." (John 20:31 ,KJ)

i. "He that believeth on the Son hath everlasting life . . . . " (John 3:36,KJ)

j. "But without faith it is impossible to please him." (Heb. 11:6,KJ)

k. John 5:24."Verily, verily, I say unto you, he that heareth my word, and believeth on me that sent me, hath everlasting life, and shall not come into condemnation; but they are passed from death unto life." (John 5:24,KJ)

l. "....and him that cometh to me I will in no wise cast out." (John 6:37,KJ)

m. "Jesus said "....except a man be born again, he cannot see the Kingdom of God." (John 3:3,KJ) Salvation!

n. "....Ye must be born again. Note: By way of the cross and Jesus grace of salvation." (John 3:7,KJ)

o. "Jesus said unto her, I am the resurrection and the life." (John 11:25,KJ)

p. "For God so loved the world, that he gave His only begotten Son, that whosoever believeth in Him should not perish, but have everlasting life." (John 3:16,KJ) This is a birth right, if we so choose.

q. Salvation: "....having this seal, the Lord knoweth them that are his. And, let everyone that nameth the name of Christ depart from iniquity." (2 Tim.2:19,KJ)

r. Romans 14:12. Salvation: "So then everyone of us shall give account of himself to God" (Rom. 14:12 KJ) Also see John 5:24.

s. "But God commendeth his love toward us, in that, while we were yet sinners, Christ died for us." (Rom. 5:8,KJ)

t. "Who his own self bore our sins in his own body on the tree." (1 Peter 2:24,KJ)

u. "....if we walk in the light, as he is in the light, we have fellowship one with the other, and the blood of Jesus Christ, his Son cleanseth us from all sin. Note: Here he speaks of brother/sisterhood in the Christian life." (1 John 1:7,KJ)

v. Acts 4:12. "Neither is there salvation in any other: for there is none other name under heaven among men, whereby we must be saved." John the Baptist could not serve as a substitute for salvation by the way of the cross. For he is not the God sent authority to grant permission of such a Holy communion. (Acts 4:12,KJ)

w. "....what must I do to be saved?" (Acts 16:30,KJ)

x. Acts 16:31."....believe on the Lord Jesus Christ, and thou shalt be saved and thy house," (Acts 16:31,KJ) Note: This is accomplished either in the secrets of our hearts or in our church of choice which is the embodiment of Jesus Christ.

y. Rev. 3:20. "Behold, I stand at the door and knock: if any man hear my voice, and open the door, I will come into him." (Rev. 3:20,KJ) in order to receive salvation we must open the door to our hearts and make the commitment to stand steadfast in his redemptive grace of us. It is by faith in our salvation that gives purpose to journey today and into the future. By God's grace we are saved and guided.

z. "Therefore, if any man is in Christ, he is a new creature." (2 Cor. 5:17,KJ)
    Note: It is our responsibility as an assignment from God to serve as witnesses to our salvation. Our redemption is

a coupling (marriage) of faith and salvation. We can not enter the Kingdom of God with out both requirements. A promise by Jesus through our faith in his spoken words, see "God's Whispering Hope." As the hymns imply, "Nearer my God to thee", Jesus is "calling" and "Amazing Grace." All integral to "The Wonder of it all." Also, as Max Lucado so amply states it, "In the Grip of Grace."

Though I express these thoughts, I fully realize my limited vision of God's Wisdom. Other than the fact that salvation is the full embodiment of Christ's love and expectations for the human race. For it is the Spirit of Christ transplanted and incubates our faith. His grace is measured through our faith and salvation. All reflective of the voice of our savior, Jesus Christ. Like our marriage to our wife/husband we are bonded together by faith and things of the heart. Our relationship to Christ is a heart to heart union, In other words, conjoined at the heart. Anything else falls short of the glory of God. For he has drawn the lines in the sands. Salvation is more than a belief, it is a pledge of allegiance to our Heavenly Father, the CEO of the entire universe. It is an oath as well as a covenant. He controls our destination. It should be pondered with great depth of thought, for it determines our future. So board the Salvation Train Line and you'll be transported safely to your destination of your choice by the navigator our Lord, Jesus Christ. Where do you get the tickets? From our savior. No charge! His grace is free.

6. Christ in the wilderness: When Christ was confronted in the wilderness (desert?) he was constantly tempted by Satan. Yet, his holiness protected him from succumbing to temptations. It gave him the strength to draw a "line" in the sand between the evil one and himself to demonstrate his genuine righteousness. Done so as to be a lesson to us.

7. On the cross: Christ hanging on the cross was more than a heart felt need to pardon our sinful nature, but to draw a "line" between death and victory over death so that we could be afforded the same privilege of victory over death that would lead us to an eternal life with our savior. Promising by salvation to draw a "line" directly to the our gate keeper, Jesus Christ,

who leads us through to see our Father in heaven. Saying, "Not my will, but thy will be done."

8. Prayer: A direct "line" of communication was established by Christ through his spirit for our benefit. There are prayers of praise and expressions of gratitude. Then there are prayers where we submit our petitions and/or supplications for his consideration. Also, there are prayers of submission. Many times there are prayers to get us through the tough times. What ever the case, he is always listening to our prayers. He is on call twenty four hours a day. Scripture: I will hear your prayers. Actually, salvation is a prayer to Jesus Christ, our savior. John 5:15 "Now this is the confidence that we have in him, that if we ask anything according to His Will, he hears us. And if we know that He hears us,whatsoever we ask, we know that we have the petitions that we have asked of Him." Matthew 21:22 "And whatsoever things you ask in prayer, believing and will receive."1 Peter 3:12 "For the eyes of the Lord are on the righteous, and His ears are open to their prayers." Phil. 4:6 "Be anxious for nothing, but in everything by prayer and supplications (petitions) with thanksgiving, let your requests be made known to God."

Now let us summarize by capsulating and internalizing the aforementioned thoughts. First is the realization that God (Christ) set the standards and requirements for salvation. Also, that we can not please God without faith. For faith leads us to the base of the cross for justification through redemption of sins and Christ's acceptance of our petitions. He hears our supplication and responds accordingly. The approach to him must be genuine and sincere. Our honesty and integrity of character will be tested and measured. For we will embark on a new journey with new dimensions. Even to the point that we'll take on a new image. Note: We were made in the image of God. By salvation we are reborn. For faith is a measurement of Christianity. Where faith carries us to the cross and into the future. Faith is our ticket to salvation. And, salvation is our ticket to live forever a life in the presence of our heavenly Father. Our heavenly Host, our Creator, our Redeemer and our care taker for life everlasting. We, too, will become Holy. Any other approaches are wasted faith. Behold, "The Wonders of Salvation!".

The antidote for boredom, anxiety, frustration and learning about God's creative genius and the grace of Jesus Christ's redemptive power is to infuse it into our thinking and release it by uttering the words of poetry or by other works of grace. Phil 2:12 "Therefore, my dear friends continue to work out your salvation. Prove to the world that we are Christians. Because it is God working in you, both in the willing and the doing." Paul is reminding the Christians in Philippi to stay focused on Jesus Christ. The Lord's Prayer says; ".....give us our daily bread". It causes us to rejoice with words, voice and good deeds. The "Wonder of it all" describes God's Greatness and compassion. The poems bear witness that a soul is working out his salvation through Christ's redemptive grace, in our pilgrimage, the power of Jesus transforms us in ways we never knew possible before. Each morning God awakes us and introduces us to the "Wonder of it all".

If we don't listen to "God's Whispering Hope" then life is meaningless. And, if we don't believe that our soul is homeward bound, then faith is worthless and futile. Our purpose for living becomes a tragedy. A dead end street, with Christ's promises being fruitless. It is our assignment and responsibility to "Draw Attention" to God's Word which fulfills not only His precepts and promises, but the interpretation of hymns sung and poems read. All of which reflects the workings of the indwelling spirit, in other words, Christ at work regardless of our inability to capture the full meaning and significance of "The Wonder of it all". The commandments tell us to love thy God with all your heart and love thy neighbor as thy self. Essentially saying, if you love me receive my love and tell your neighbors of My way of salvation. Behold, "The Wonders of Salvation." 2 Corinthians 8:11 "....but now you must also complete the doing of it; that as there was a readiness to desire it, so then also may it be a completion out of what you have." Christ reminds us that salvation is an entitlement, but you have to stand before him and ask for it. It is a prayer of supplication.

The bottom line: Jesus loves us and he is calling. So get on the line and call him. Behold, "The Wonders of Salvation".

SIN IN CHRIST

1.   None of us can imagine, nor thoroughly comprehend the significance and magnitude of what Christ accomplished for us on the cross. Especially the agony of his sacrifice. Here are some examples.
    a.   Pain, grief, sorrow and disappointment.
        6 billion in the world today.
        4 billion people in the past
        10 billion people in the history of humanity.
    b.   Christ suffered every sin for all of humanity past, present and future.
    c.   How many of us could with stand that amount of agony?
    d.   So often we take that for granted.

2.   Christ lived with sin.
    a.   He was man in the flesh.
    b.   So that he could withstand, experience, observe and witness every temptation humanity struggled with. otherwise he would not know the reason for hanging on the cross.
    c.   He was subject to the same temptations as us.
    d.   That was precisely the reason for being nailed to the cross.

3.   Christ groans for us.
    a.   The Bible tells us that each time we sin, he groans.
    b.   Yet, he loves us enough to forgive our trespasses.

Scripture: " He made Him who knew no sin to "be sin for us." (2 Cor. 5:21 KJ)

"So Christ was once offered to bear the sins of many; and unto them that look for him shall he appear the second time without sin unto salvation."

(Heb. 9:28,KJ)" What shall we say then? Is the law sin? God forbid. Nay, I had not known sin, but by the law..."

(Rom, 7:7,KJ) "....Christ liveth in me; and the life which I now live in the flesh I live by the faith of the Son of God, who loved me, and gave Himself for me." (Gal. 2:17,KJ)

4. Why do I want salvation through Christ?
   a. To express my gratitude.
   b. To see my family and friends in heaven.
   c. To fortify my faith.
   d. To live in hope of an extended life beyond today.
   e. To be living in Christ be a witness for the glory of God.
   f. To cash in on a treasure beyond measure.

HYMN: AMAZING GRACE

Amazing grace ! How sweet the sound,
that saved a wretch like me.
I once was lost but now am found,
was blind, but now I see.

Twas grace that taught my heart to fear,
and grace my fears relieved.
How precious did that grace appear,
the hour I first believed.

The Lord has promised good to me;
His word my hope secure.
He will my shield and portion be,
as long as life endures.

Through many dangers, toils and snares,
I have already come.
Tis grace hath brought me safe thus far,
and grace will lead me home.

The Celebration Hymnal

A HEART FOR JESUS

Because we are diversified people we are beckoned to his calling in multiple ways. Though he walks beside us without making footprints in the sand we can sense his presence. He is the shadow that moves with us. Because of God's expectations of us he does and will draw lines in the sand separating us from Him. We are separated by our human nature. But because of his immeasurable love and grace he will grant us the honor and privilege to walk on the side of salvation. Making us a special people in his kingdom for ever. He is our heavenly Father with wisdom, understanding and mercy. I can't think of a more appropriate hymn to this theme than "Softly and tenderly Jesus is calling."

SOFTLY AND TENDERLY

Softly and tenderly Jesus is calling
Calling for you and me.
See, on the portals He's waiting and watching,
Watching for you and me.

Why should we tarry when Jesus is pleading,
Pleading for you and for me?
Why should we linger and heed not His mercies,
Mercies for you and for me.

Time is now fleeting, the moments are passing,
Passing from you and from me.
Shadows are gathering; death's night is coming,
Coming for you and for me.

O for the wonderful love His has promised,
Promised for you and for me.
Though we have sinned, He has mercy and pardon,
Pardon for you and for me.

Come home, come home. You who are weary, come home.
Earnestly, tenderly Jesus is calling,
Calling, "O Sinner, come home!"

The Celebration Hymnal

He benevolently hugs us and tell us, "You are forgiven and therefore become a child of God. All Christians who have that trust and faith in Christ's promises can with confidence and assurance can this birth right.

How can we express our gratitude and praise for having been afforded such an opportunity? One possibility is to explore "The Wonder of it All!" To willfully establish a mind-set to venture into and examine the blessings the heavenly Father has bestowed on us past, present and future. If we approach this assignment with an open mind and heart it will flood our souls with surprises beyond our imagination. For God has and will bless us abundantly. However, to seek we must search, identify and acknowledge all the wonders at our threshold of a Christian life. It will feed our desires and give inspiration to march into the future with excitement and anticipation.

Our minds can be trained to recognize God's grace. For the aspiring Christian it is a spiritual dream come true. For to see the wonders of God we must first read and let our minds imagine the creative genius of God. It fosters dreams and visionary thoughts that fulfill and satisfy our anticipation of salvation.

To set idle and be dormant in our thinking, it becomes a barrier to the door of that wonderland. Once we enter we do not see a land of destruction, but endless possibilities. Therefore, realizing that we all have a purpose in God's Master Plan. To proceed with visionary thoughts sets the stage and prepares our heart, minds and soul for the journey ahead with Christ at the helm. It will give us a more realistic insight and interpretation that will enable us to acquire a grander view and appropriate appreciation for the providence of God. Our spiritual transformation into that image is dependent on three things; willingness, thinking and acceptance of God's way. Jesus made it very clear that we are to change our image to be seen by the Father of our being. It is an on going revival process forever changing. Change made it possible to step over that line of demarcation scribed in the sand by our heavenly teacher to live a life with the Holy One for eternity. Therefore, "We must take captive every thought to make it obedient to Christ." (2 Cor. 10:3) By entering into this adventure it should yield to us The Great Revelation." That Christ is our Savior! Also, the revelation that there exists "God's Whispering Hope."

But we must initiate the need and desire to draw back the curtain to such a drama. Once we tune our senses to the whisper of God's voice to our conscience we eventually realize that God is not silent. We begin to see God at work all around us. Not only in creation but in the lives of people we associate with. We ultimately come face to face with the conclusion that the Spirit of the Almighty One of all things is not only present around us, but can dwell within us simultaneously. It gives us the fortitude to stand tall in the conviction of Christ's image. It gives us the confidence to rely on the Christian faith. It gives us the power that when internalized it prompts us to accomplish things beyond our expectations. The writing of this book is an example. It has fostered the courage to share it and weave it into the lives of other people.

Spiritual alignment means to respond to the call of Jesus and comply with his sincere request and invitation. He is the authority to direct ourselves to the cross of salvation. It should feed our ideals and spiritual needs. Those who lack this vision can't develop the insight to look beyond themselves. We have an tendency to lock ourselves in a closet. However, Jesus can open the door to engage immeasurable hope and promises. Hope that carries us through the rigors of each day, each month and each year. It unleashes the spirit that provides the driving force that propels us into the countless unknowns in our life. It expands our vision and prepares us not only to see into the future as well as to define more clearly our faith. There is always an incessant need to discover, understand and apply what constitutes our faith. The content of this book hopefully emphasizes that view point. We must expand our vision, stir our conscience, widen our Christian purpose to ignite our imagination as it pertains to not only God's significance in our lives, but to reciprocate by internalizing the spirit of Christ's message. A message that all can be well in our soul and give it back to him with a smile. To grasp the moment to express our gratitude for his gracious gifts. It is available to all who trust in the Lord. Knowledge helps us to shape the future with an applause for our creators will. It is not a fantasy that fades away and leads us down a path to nothingness. God will be there to accept us into His majestic heavenly world. There is a great surprise in store for the faithful. The grace of Christ and faith shall lead us to the threshold of the doorway to his home land. Yes, it is a profound reality that our Lord predestined and presents to us that option in our life. In the mean time we are on a voyage into "The Wonder of it All." Faith and cultivation of the spirit are inseparable. The truth of God's message is always before us, even unto the end time. The truth forges ahead of us preparing the way. The end time shall be a test of our confidence in Christ's words. It will be a blend of faith, love, trust and gracious endurance that delivers us into the hands of our maker for ever "He Leadth The Way!" A revelation and spiritual dream come true and forged personally by God himself. We shall come to know in person the redemptive power of our savior. However, we should be cautious not to let the intellectual mind falsely introduce us into that realm of being, for that is an impossibility. We must thoroughly and fully accept that it is the grace of our Lord that controls our destination. Intellect alone will not induct us into his Hall of Fame. It is the magnitude of God's redemptive power that provides the reward. The significance of it is almost beyond comprehension. A treasure beyond our imagination. The corner stone of Christian life today and forever. We shall awake to that scene when we pass from our earthly place to our heavenly dwelling place. Imagine the glorious smile on Christ's face when we arrive. It was foretold by him for our salvation and benefit. We will not need to buy a travel ticket for the passage, it is free by the saving grace of our High Priest, Jesus Christ.

Appreciating our maker can only be established by internalizing God's Greatness. It requires emersion of thought and imagination. It requires more than just reading the scriptures. There is the requirement of solitude, quietude, patience, serenity and a genuine sense of purpose. It takes time to put the puzzle of faith together. Reflection is essential to focus and infuse the spirit into our learning processes. The Bible is not all we know about the creative genius of our creator. It brings forth a sensitivity for God's creative design and an awareness of what he has given us. Even our intuitiveness gives credence to our discoveries inherent to living our lives on earth. God is the provider and Holy Market Place for all things. It provides the stimulus for earthly survival as well as spiritual survival. Pondering these wonderments is a key element to living a productive and purpose driven Christian life. Not to, puts us on the road of self-destruction. Paul reminds us that our objective is to work toward the goal and the discoveries along the way to fortify our approach. Yes, along the way we'll encounter disappointments, thus enabling us to discover our deficiencies. So, therefore, preparation of mind, heart and spirit is vital. Thus giving justification to our Christian dignity. Otherwise, life can be mundane without spiritual reward and gratification. This can be avoided by letting God's faithfulness, love and grace guide our course. Without Him, nothing exists. Without Him there isn't any hope. Without Him faith becomes meaningless. To get spiritual nourishment and strength we must feed on and digest what God has given us. This implies that we are to compel ourselves to open the book to the wonders of God's grace, in other words, gaze with awe into the crystal ball of "The Wonder of it All." God wrote His letters to us, now take time to reciprocate by writing letters to Him about your discoveries. He will read your journal. Your mind will be changed forever. It should be a planned and necessary mission. It is faith in action and delivers us from the bondage of "So What!" Embrace the freedom to soar like an eagle and praise the kingdom in which we participate on a daily basis. To engage is really a form of worship. There will be a manifestation of the spirit that will fill the heart with joy. But it must be a genuine faithful act to accomplish this task. "Good Luck!" Appropriate to this chain of thoughts are the words "The most beautiful things in the world can not be touched. They must be felt with the heart." Remember "Jesus loves me, this I know."

GOD'S DELIGHT

Can you imagine the joy in God's heart when he held in his hands and released a butterfly forour enjoyment?

Can you imagine the gladness in His heart when he heard the voices of the song birds?

Can you image the rejoicing in His heart when he let the doe run in a field with her fawn?

Can you imagine the excitement when He saw the colorful flowers in the meadow?

Can you imagine the delight in His voice when his Son tells him "I have redeemed another soul?"

Can you imagine the smile on His face when he sees us face to face in his heavenly domain?

"Delight thyself in the Lord; and he shall give thee the desires of thine heart." (Psalm 37:4, KJ)

"I press toward the mark for the prize of the high calling of God in Christ Jesus." (Phil. 3:14, KJ)

"Where there is not vision the people perish " (Proverbs 29:18, KJ)

"So teach us to number our days, that we may apply our hearts unto wisdom." (Psalm 90:12, KJ)

"Being justified freely by His grace through the redemption that is in Jesus Christ." (Rom. 3:24,KJ)

"But God commendth His love toward us, in that, while we were yet sinners, Christ died for us." (Rom. 5:8,KJ)

"....but the gift of God is eternal life through Jesus Christ our Lord." (Rom.6:23,KJ)

"For whosoever shall call upon the name of the Lord shall be saved." (Rom.l0:13,KJ)

"But as many as received him, to them gave he power to become the sons of God, even to them that believe in his name." (John 1:12,KJ)

"Whosoever shall confess me before men, him will I confess also before my Father which is in heaven." (Matt. 10:13,KJ)

"Blessed are they that keep his testimonies and seek him with the whole heart." (Psalmll9:2,KJ)

"Go home to they friends, and tell them how great things the Lord hath had compassion on thee."(Mark5:19,KJ)

"You, O Eternal Trinity, are a deep sea into which,
The more I enter, the more I find,
And the more I find, the more I seek."
St. Catherine of Siena

FRUITS OF THY SPIRIT

Dear Jesus,

Thank you for the fruit of thy spirit,
peace, joy and good to all.
These attitudes harbored with great merit.
One remains, "Love" supreme to all,
its acclaim cheerfully hail.

Love unclaimed is a buried treasure,
useless, it won't bear fruit.
Love proclaimed in fullest measure,
helping others in full pursuit.

Love is an attitude of great potency,
its power removes complacency.
Love destroys greed, hate and war,
open they heart and let it freely soar.

Love, plant the seed and watch the growth,
in the downtrodden hope it restoreth.
Love others and show kindness,
help them find happiness.

A smile to remove sadness.
Love will return to your heart,
to fill it with gladness.
Knowing you have given your part.

Peace instills good cheer,
with no fear we can onward peer.
Goodwill, your fortune for sharing,
your spirit shows the caring. Joy replaces sorrow,
and brightens tomorrow.

Peace in your soul,
giving joy to our stroll.
Goodwill spread throughout the nation,
these loving thoughts bring satisfaction.

Day to day love by the fruit of the spirit.
Thank Jesus and praise it with gratitude.
Christ's love is the ultimate sacrifice,
a gift beyond price.

Around the world spread His will,
so that "ALL" live in peace, joy and goodwill.
Thank you Jesus!

RG

MY MORNING GLORY

Early morning, time to wake and to rise,
to the window to witness the sunrise.
What a pleasant surprise.
On the horizon there is a radiant glow,
it shineth through window with gentle flow.
There too, I see creatures awaken,
another day God has not forsaken.

Then I see a trellis of morning glory,
each flower on display in natures gallery.
Now they, too, awaken,
petals open and sunlight inward taken.
Its energy fills their need,
reason, to produce more seed.
This morning they show their glory,
arise each morning filled with joy.

Each morning my soul to rise,
God's presence to realize.
In our spirit gently flow,
filling life with a brilliant glow.
My spirit now has awaken,
knowing God has not forsaken.

God's letters I read,
fulfilling a special need.
Christ's assurance is the prize,
that shouldn't be a surprise.
My soul and my spirit He feeds,
blessed with His gracious deeds.
A new life guaranteed.
This morning God showed His glory,
God is my morning glory.

RG

Note: This poem is not to imply that I am spiritually awake each morning. If that were true, then I would be a Saint. With humility and self examination I realize my limitations and short comings. However, God admonished us to worship Him and praise each day of our life. Our human faults and circumstances tests our capability of measuring out the Holy Spirit that Christ gave to dwell in our souls. Each day we need Christ to give us hope and strength to cope. We must rely on that hope.

A HEART OF LOVE

From where does love originate?
Given to us as a choice.
It is more than just fate,
it comes from God's voice.

It is to have and behold,
a gift of a special art.
It spreads as life unfolds,
helping to serve a special part.

It is essential for a Christian life,
it is God's will at work.
His grace through us uplifts,
where it goes it leaves a special mark.

What is the gift of love?
It is part of our Christian faith.
Given to others, free as a bird,
like the winds that blow.
Into the hearts of others,
we lift them with spirit low.

We are asked to plant special seeds,
that will grow into joyous deeds.
Lighting a glow in their hearts,
as our love we impart.

Serving our Lord and gracehood,
living in brother/sisterhood.
Making us dearer and nearer to our Lord,
love granted on his accord.
Surely this act we can afford,
as our cup of faith is poured.

This is our duty as Christian's,
to lend a helping hand.
for we live together on this land.
Forging ahead with God's heart of love.

RG

"And let us consider one another in order
to stir up love and good.." (Heb. 10:24)

GRACE RIVER FLOW

By grace we were given life,
a gift beyond measure.
Yet, there is a bigger treasure,
through Christ, eternal life,
There, by faith, are such pleasures.

By grace we were given abundance,
respond with joy and dance.
On His earth we toil,
planting seeds in the soil.
Oh, but it is only a temporary glance.

By grace we were given nature,
day by day we have a grand tour.
Wildlife abounds, especially the flowers,
through out vision they uplift with power.

By grace we were given family and friends,
on their love we have come to depend.
Always there to encourage when in illness,
praying and wishing for wellness.

By grace we were given love,
in our hearts, God endowed.
Woven into all relationships,
release it, let it be free as a dove.
Encompassing us like a shroud,
there in lays Christ's friendship.

By grace we are redeemed,
making us a Christian team.
A promise from the cross,
even though we are tempest tossed.

By grace we are given the Spirit,

through Christ it is our birth right.
To have and behold this day forth,
to our Heavenly Father we have worth.

By grace we become His messenger,
a Christ child born in a manger.
Our deliverance through salvation,
a guaranteed promise through his certification.
Words spoken by his voice,
in that we should rejoice.

By grace we were given faith,
yes, it is this truth we must hath.
It is ours to have, granted by a reliable source,
a Christian theme to keep us on course.

By grace there is a reward,
our Savior, Christ, guides us toward.
Then at the Grace River end,
where Christ to his Father, us he sends.
Understand, embrace it and go,
there is a treasure at the end of the flow.
There you'll find a radiant glow.

                                        RG

CHAPTER 11:

THE GREATEST GIFT EVER

"This is what God told us: God has given us eternal life, and this life is in His Son." (1 John 5:11,KJ)

STANDING ON HIS PROMISES

Standing on the promises of Christ my King!
Through eternal ages let His praises ring;
"Glory in the highest" I will shout and sing,

Standing on the promises that can not fail,
When the howling storms of doubt and fear assail,
By the living Word of God I shall prevail,

Standing on the promises, I now can see,
Perfect, present cleansing in the blood for me;
Standing in the liberty where Christ makes free,

Standing on the promises of Christ, the Lord,
Bound to Him eternally by love's strong cord,
Over coming daily with the Spirit's Sword,

Standing on the promises, I can not fail,
Listening every moment to the Spirit's call,
Resting in my Savior as my All in All.

The Celebration Hymnal

I will never leave you, nor forsake you." (Heb. 13:5,KJ)
"I am with you always, even unto the end of the world." (Matt. 28:20,KJ)
"....for so an entrance will be supplied to you abundantly into the everlasting Kingdom of our Lord and Savior, Jesus Christ." (2 Peter 1:11, KJ)

HYMN: AMAZING GRACE

Amazing grace! How sweet the sound,
That saved a wretch like me!
I once was lost but now an found;
Was blind, but now I see.

I was grace that taught my heart to fear,
and grace my fears relieved,
How precious did that grace appear,
The hour I first believed.

The Lord has promised good to me;
His word my hope secure.
He will my shield and portion be,
As long as life endures.

Through many dangers, toils and snares,
I have already come.
Tis grace hath brought me safe thus far,
And grace will lead me home.

When we've been there ten thousand years.
Bright shinning as the sun,
We've no less days to sing,
God's praise than when we first begun.

The Celebration Hymnal

"And, having made peace through the blood of his cross, by him to reconcile all things unto himself; by him, I say, whether they be things in the earth, or things in heaven." (Col. 1:20,KJ)

"Now the Lord is that Spirit: and when the Spirit of the Lord is, there is liberty. But we all, with open face beholding as a glass the glory of the Lord, are changed into the same image from glory to glory, even as by the Spirit of the Lord." (2 Cor. 3:17,18,KJ)

"And all things are of God, who hath reconciled us to himself by Jesus Christ, and hath given us the ministry of reconciliation." (2 Cor. 5:18 KJ)

"...shall he not much more clothe you, O ye of little faith." (Matt. 6:30,KJ)

"....ye are risen with him through the faith of the operation of God, who hath raised him from the dead." (Col. 2:12,KJ)

HE DWELLS IN OUR HEARTS

The image of Christ is invisible today. Therefore, that creates a perplexing problem for many people. Sometimes we feel that he has forsaken us. Being invisible, how do we know he lives today? It is a refrain that puzzles us sometimes and warps our thinking. If we can't see him, how do we realize his redemptive powers? He can't look in our eyes and say "You are now saved and have become a son of God." We can't see him to experience receiving the certificate (gift) of eternal life. A certificate that guarantees our sins have been forgiven. He can't hug us and give us assurance of his grace. It is a matter of faith and developing an appropriate perspective.

There is a hymn in the hymnal that may help us gain some insight. It is titled "He Lives." It identifies the fact that Christ is our risen savior and his spirit dwells throughout humanity. It further states that is loving, kind and filled with grace. In addition, it clarifies that he can declare our salvation. We see his love indwelling others who display grace in their works, there tender loving care and the willingness to sacrifice their time. His spirit guides us through our journey and troubled episodes in life, giving us hope. We must envision that he exists. If Jesus is not alive today, then our prayers are worthless. Also, our eternal hope has vanished. Furthermore, if he isn't with us in our daily affairs, then he lied to us. Because he is the Anointed One, the Son of God and the resurrected one baptized in the Holy Spirit, his words can be trusted beyond doubt.

> In our hearts he dwells,
>   Letting us know all is well,
>   Granted through God's will.
>
> In us, his grace is unveiled,
>   He asks us to be still,
>   A promise he fulfilled.
>
> To humanity he is a Savior,
>   Churches ministers, hymns tell the story.

Around the world his spirit he does pour.
Ours to grasp for his glory.

Yes, for this we should rejoice,
Even if we can't hear his voice.
He extends his redemptive hands,
Throughout the lands.

Just as God planned,
Listen and see His glorious plan.
Available to the whole human race.
From our Lord with grace.

GOD IS NEAR

How do we know God is near,
as we daily go our way?
What possesses us to think He is there?
Or, do we say he is here?

I see Him in all that surrounds,
I see Him in you and me.
Everywhere he abounds,
all we have to do is look and see.

In our hearts he is found,
to us he'll forever be.
To us he'll set the sails,
even when we are frail.

Yes, he is never far away,
united with every heart.
Trust in Him, day after day,
God is near and will never depart.

To this dream take hold,
for your faith he will mold.

RG

"The Lord is close to everyone who prays
to him. To all who truly pray to Him." (Psalm 17:6)

HYMN: HE LIVES

I serve a risen Savior,
He's in the world today;
I know that He is living,
what ever men may say,
I see His hand of mercy,
I hear His voice of cheer,
And just the time I need Him,
He's always near.

In all the world around me,
I see His loving care;
And though my heart grows weary,
I never will despair.
I know that He is leading,
through all the stormy blast;
The day of His appearing will come at last.

Rejoice, rejoice, O Christian,
lift up your voice and sing,
Eternal halleluiah,
to Jesus Christ, the King !
The hope of all who seek Him,
the help of all who find,
None other is so loving,
so Good and Kind.

Christ Jesus lives today !
He walks (spirit) with me and
talks (spirit) with me during life's way.
He gives salvation to impart!
You ask me how I know He lives ?
He lives within my heart.

The Celebration Hymnal

THE MAGNANIMOUS TREE

Take a meditation walk today,
walk with Christ on this day.
His spirit follows along the way,
then I noticed a tree beside the pathway.

Christ, I asked. What is that tree?
He said, "That's the magnanimous tree."
You are walking in the New Garden of Eden,
its fruit is not forbidden.

Beautiful blossoms in wind sway,
in awe I briefly stay.
Its blossoms radiant glow,
it is Christ's love free to flow.

It's springtime with flowers in bloom,
this tree year round blooms.
Take its fruit and eat from the mag tree,
Christ's spirit as a gift to thee.

But Christ, the fruit on branches are not the same,
He said, I am to blame.
The fruit of faith;
Eyes fixed to the future,
your trust and hope it will forever nurture.

The fruit of joy;
A spirit glowing with happiness.
A spirit to wash away sadness.

The fruit of peace;
God's Will to live in harmony,
holding hands while walking in unity.
Like music at a concert,
all singing in concert.

The fruit of goodwill;
Kindness to those in need,
fill a fear with gladness as a daily deed.

The fruit of long suffering;
God's spirit provides the endurance,
through pain, tragedy and grievance.

The spirit of self-control;
Your anger, your hate and your spite,
your temper subdue before you strike.
No curse in God's eye is right,
keep forgiveness forever in sight.

The fruit of gentleness;
Courteous to others and don't be harsh,
be patient for your love will tarnish.

The fruit of love;
This fruit is supreme to all,
Christ's special gift if you recall.

With fruit in soul to reside,
Christ said, "We must abide".

Now go forth and plant the seed,
a magnanimous tree for all to feed.

At strolls end with Chrit's love abiden,
walking in the New Garden of Eden.

RG

REJOICING

When God created the universe, He rejoiced.

When God created life on earth, He rejoiced.

He was pleased when He looked at the animals, fish, birds, plants, He rejoiced.

When He created man and woman, He rejoiced.

Then they betrayed His loving gift, saddened was His rejoicing.

Then God made a way to reclaim His children.
For each soul he reclaims, He rejoices.

Then He gave humankind a choice,
Reject Me or follow Me, then I'll rejoice.

In salvation there is rejoicing,
for it unites us with God, rejoice.

He promises everlasting life,
Our hearts should over-flow with rejoicing.

Always remember that it pleases God and
restores His rejoicing.

Rejoice, rejoice, rejoice, for it is God's Will.
Our hope in heaven, He will fulfill.

For rejoicing is found in the book of life,
It is found in "The Wonder of it all".

                                        RG

Paul said "Rejoice in the Lord always, Again, I say, rejoice !"
(Phil. 4:4, JH)

Psalm 100: "Make a joyful shout to the Lord, all the lands !"
(Psalm 4:4,KJ)
Serve the Lord with gladness;
Come before His presence with singing.
Know that the Lord, He is God;
It is He who made us and not we ourselves.
We are His people and the sheep of His pasture.
Enter into His gates with thanksgiving,
And into His courts with praise,
Be thankful to Him and bless His name.
For the Lord is good;
His mercy is everlasting,
And His truth endures to all generations".

"Make a joyful shout to God, all the earth!" (Psalm 66:1,KJ)
Sing out the honor of His name;
Make His praise glorious. Say to God
"How awesome are Your works !".

Note: The title and context of this book surrounds that acclaim.

"And my soul shall be joyful in the Lord." (Psalm 35:9,KJ)

"Oh come, let us sing to the Lord!" (Psalm 95:2,KJ)
Let us come before His presence with thanksgiving.
Let us shout joyfully to Him in psalms".

In Christ we all have our individual psalm to sing, whether it be writing hymns, poems, stories to be told as a means to witness or design things to bring recognition to our Lord. Hopefully, this collection of thoughts will promote rejoicing. Like the eagle, let the spirit reign free so we all can enjoy it.

A HEART OF LOVE

From where does love originate?
Given to us as a choice.
It is more than just fate,
it comes from God's voice.

It is to have and behold,
a gift of a special art.
It spreads as life unfolds,
helping to serve a special part.

It is essential for a Christian life,
it is God's will at work.
His grace through us uplifts,
where it goes it leaves a special mark.

What is the gift of love?
It is part of our Christian faith.
Given to others, free as a bird,
like the winds that blow.
Into the hearts of others,
we lift them with spirit low.

We are asked to plant special seeds,
that will grow into joyous deeds.
Lighting a glow in their hearts,
as our love we impart.

Serving our Lord and gracehood,
living in brother/sisterhood.
Making us dearer and nearer to our Lord,
love granted on his accord.
Surely this act we can afford,
as our cup of faith is poured.

This is our duty as Christian's, to lend a helping hand.
for we live together on this land.
Forging ahead with God's heart of love.
RG

"And let us consider one another in order
to stir up love and good.." (Heb. 10:24)

LET ALL THINGS NOW LIVING
(Hymn)

Let all things now living,
a song of thanksgiving to the creator triumphantly raise;
Who fashioned and made us,
protected and stayed us,
Who still guides us onto the end of our days.

God's banners are over us.
His light goes before us,
A pillar of fire shinning forth in the night.
Till shadows have vanished,
and darkness is banished,
As forward we travel from light into light.

His law He enforces;
The stars in their courses,
and seen in its orbit abundantly shine.
The hills and the mountains,
the rivers and fountains,
    - The depth of ocean proclaims Him divine, Alleluia !

We, too, should be voicing,
our love and rejoicing;
With glad adoration a song let us raise.
Till all things now living,
unite in thanksgiving,
"To God in the highest, honor and praise."
                   The Celebration Hymnal

CHAPTER 12:

LET THERE BE PEACE ON EARTH

Let there be peace on earth and let it begin with me,
Let there be peace on earth, the peace that was meant to be,
with God as our Father, we are family.
Let us walk with each other in perfect harmony,
Let peace begin with me, let this be the moment now,
with every step I take, let this be my solemn vow,
To take each moment and live each moment in peace
eternally.
Let there be peace on earth, and let it begin with me.

THE LOST TREASURE "PEACE"

"P"   PEOPLE searching for a golden treasure,
       waiting for its fullest measure.

"E"   EVILS from which to escape,
       spreading hope across the landscape.

"A"   ASPERATIONS of heartfelt need,
       as we walk spread the seed.

"C"   All CIVILIZATION in harmony,
       free from evils agony.

"E"   Oh, the ECTASY and the rejoice,
       it dwells in our hearts as a choice.

The Peace Dove we reach to hold,
then frightened away, hopes foiled.
How does man break the evil chain ?
The shackles which prevent peaceful reign.

In Brotherhood and Grace-hood we should bask,
the pursuit of ghostly task.
Peace grows from the heart,
crafted daily as an art.

Precipitating like rain, this peaceful grace,
knitting God's Will in woven lace.
Divided people walking hand-in-hand,
a chain of "PEACE" uniting all the lands.

RG

OPEN THINE EYES TO PEACE

History recounts man's evil seeds,
Oh, those dastardly deeds.
War, prejudice, hatred, vengeance, greed,
the failure to follow the Peace Creed.

An attitude of tit-for-tat, an eye for an eye,
fuels havoc, then we wonder why ?
Anger, grudges, distrust wounds the heart,
wounds that never heal or depart.

Resentment smolders like hot ashes,
ready to ignite more clashes.
A malignant disease of contagious infection,
borne on winds from generation to generation.

Nations of people in a strangle hold,
struggling in vain to release its hold.
How does man break the chain ?
The shackles which prevent peaceful reign.

People wearing the armor of distrust,
as fears inward thrust.
Indifferences which compromises,
and tarnishes our will and our promises.

Nations of people headed toward doom,
not knowing what they are doing.
How do we shed the evils of mankind ?
those faults which makes us blind.

Oh, the joy to escape this gloom,
let us plant the "PEACE" flower and watch it bloom.
Grace, hail the power of this word,
our gifts to the world. A belief in this power,
over the world should tower.

A theme central to our living faith,
peace dispensed as we goeth.
We the people are the dispensers of Peace,
our will to unite the human race.

Our will through grace,
the world should embrace.
Quenching the thirst for freedom.
Hurray ! Peace throughout the Kingdom.

Yes, there is a way to reconciliation,
rather than angers retaliation. God's Will is to make peace,
behold the power of love when evil cease. God's Will guides
us to liberation, world peace, Oh, the jubilation. Forging
the Glory of God, as forward we trod. Fulfillment of God's
Creed,

> No more vengeance.
> No more prejudice.
> No more hatred.
> No more greed.
> The central thought is forgiveness,
> An act preceded by willingness.
>
> RG

This poem was inspired by the following prayers:
Lord's Prayer; "Forgive us our trespasses as we forgive those who trespass
against us."

A little girl's prayer; Lord, keep the good people nice and make the bad
people nicer."

Jesus said, "For if you forgive men their trespasses, your heavenly Father
will also you.but if you do not forgive men their trespasses, neither will
your Father forgive your trespasses".

"Jesus, who gave Himself for our sins, that He might deliver us from
this present evil world according to the Will of God our Father." (Gal.
1:4,KJ)

GOD'S WILL

'It is God's Will !"
How often this phrase is misused.
Misfortune strikes us down,
then we chant in bold resound.
"It's God's Will !" thoroughly confused,
God's Will clearly abused,
In troubled mind we reply,
asking God the question, "Why ?"

Moses said "God, why have you brought troubles on
these people and, you have not rescued your people at all ?."

Jesus said, "God, why have you forsaken me ?"
Hanging on the cross for all.

When in grief despair it instills,
"Is it really God's Will?"

A child dies, then we say, "It's God's Will !
In sickness we suffer. Then we say, "It's God's Will".
Hundreds killed, Then we say, "It's God's Will !"

Such folly this misuse of God's intentions,
calling God killer, murderer, deliverance of misfortune.
Misunderstanding God's intentional will,
altered by man's circumstantial will.
God's intention is for good health and good will,
in our soul His love to fulfill.
Lean not on your understanding,
but lean on God's love everlasting.

Jesus said, "It is not the will of your Father in heaven that one
of these little ones should perish".
To this promise we hold and cherish.
Often we shout, "God where are you ?".

Christ said, "Your Father has not forgotten you."
Jesus also said, "So that in Me you may have peace,
in this world you will have troubles,
but take heart, I have overcome the world troubles,
be still and have faith, rest in peace."

When dwelling in the dungeon of doubt,
reaping the unfairness of life.
Give us the strength to be stout,
to conquer grief and strife.

Paul said, "Rejoice in the Lord always"
troubles we face through our days.
Our faith may waiver and sway,
remember, Jesus is with us always.

First there was God's "Intentional Will."
Mankind produces "Circumstantial Will."
In the end there is "God's Ultimate Will."
God teach me to "Understand Thy Will."
Thy Will be done on earth as it is in heaven,
God, "Carry our soul in our grieven."

RG

GOD'S WILL THROUGH GRACE

History recounts man's evil seeds,
Oh, those dastardly deeds.
War, prejudice, hatred, vengeance, greed,
the failure to follow God's creed.

An attitude of tit-for-tat, an eye for an eye,
fuels havoc, then we wonder why.
Anger, grudges, distrust wound the heart,
wounds that never heal or depart.

Resentment smolders like hot ashes,
ready to ignite more clashes.
A malignant disease of contagious infection,
borne on winds, generation to generation.

Nations of people in a stranglehold,
struggling in vain to release its hold.
How does man break the chain ?
The shackles which prevent God's reign.
People wearing the armor of distrust,
as fears inward thrust.

Political rhetoric which compromises,
tarnishes God's Will and His promises.
Nations of people headed toward doom,
Jesus said, "For they know not what they are doing."

How do we shed the evils of mankind ?
Those faults which make us blind.
Oh, the joy to escape this gloom,
let us plant the "Grace" flower and watch it bloom.

Grace, hail the power of this word,
God's gift to the world.
Oh, the thirst for its nourishment,
a yearning faith with grace embodiment.

A belief in a higher power,
over the world should tower.
A theme central to Christian Faith,
grace dispensed as we pray.

We the people are the dispersers of grace,
God's Will uniting the human race.
God's Will through grace,
the world should embrace.

Recall the hymn, "Amazing Grace",
the spirit of tomorrow to face.
Quenching the thirst for freedom,
hurray ! Peace throughout the Kingdom.

Yes, there is a way to reconciliation,
rather than angers retaliation.
God's Will is to make peace,
behold the power of love when evil cease.

God's Will guides us to liberation,
World peace. Oh, the jubilation.
Forging the Glory of God,
as forward we trod.

Fulfillment of God's Creed,
No more vengeance.
No more prejudice.
No more hatred.
No more greed.

The central thought is forgiveness,
an act preceded by willingness.

RG

This poem was inspired by the following prayers:

Lord's Prayer: "Forgive us our trespasses as we forgive those who trespass against us."

A little girls prayer: "Lord, keep the good people nice and make the bad people nicer."

Jesus said, "For if you forgive men their trespasses, your heavenly Father Will also forgive you. But if you do not forgive men their trespasses, neither will your Father forgive your trespasses."

"Jesus, who give Himself for our sins, that He might deliver us from this present evil world according to the will of God our Father." (Gel. 1:4,KJ)

PEACE THROUGH GRACE

What is grace ? You should ask,
in its meaning we should bask.
Man's evils let it rot away,
from God's Will, then led astray.

A world deaf and blind to grace,
yet, this word we should embrace.
Grace is the art of forgiveness,
a bridge connecting Christ to sinfulness.

For there we find release,
repentance instills the peace.
It transcends all the virtues,
and casts a joyous hue.

Grace grows from the heart,
crafted daily as an art.
What is the cost ? Free of charge,
God's eternal gift to small and large.

To wash and purify our soul,
God's baptism as through life we stroll.
Grace is like the sun, free to all;
Christ's promise if you recall.

Like the flowers on the hillside.
The breeze that touches our face.
The rise and setting sun.
The vision we see with our eyes.
And the birds in the sky.

God is the taproot of the vine,
the branches are all people intertwined.
The leaves are our extended hands,
reaching to all the lands.
Offering the fruit of Grace,
and the spirit to embrace.

To love is to embody grace-hood
all people living in brotherhood.
When forgiveness reigns,
love will precipitate like rain.

Bathing the earth in peaceful Grace,
knitting God's Will in a woven lace.
Divided people walking hand-in-hand,
chains of grace binding all the lands.

RG

These thoughts were inspired by :

The Lord sayeth "Peace I leave with you, my peace I give to you, not as the world giveth, give I unto you." (John 14:27,KJ)

"And the peace of God, which surpasses all comprehension shall guard your hearts and your minds in Christ Jesus." (Phil. 4:7, KJ)

Hymn: Amazing Grace

Book: "What's so amazing about grace?" by Phillip Yancy

Book: "In The Grip of Grace." by Max Lucado

HYMN: GREAT IS THY FAITHFULNESS

Great is they faithfulness,
O God, my Father;
There is no shadow of turning with Thee,
Thou changest not;
Thy compassions, they fail not.
As Thou hast been,
Thou forever wilt be.

Summer and winter,
and spring time and harvest,
sun, moon, stars in their courses above,
Join with all nature in manifold witness,
to they great faithfulness, mercy and love.

Pardon for sin and a peace that endureth,
They own dear presence to cheer and to guide.
Strength for today and bright hope for tomorrow,
blessings all mine with ten thousand besides.
Great is they faithfulness.

Words; Thomas O. Chisholm
Music: William M. Runyan
C 1923, Red. 1951 Hope Publishing Company
Carol Stream, IL 60188.
All rights erserved. Used by permission.
Reprinted under license #65475

The Glorious Sunset of Christian Life

CHAPTER 13:

A GLORIOUS SUNSET

Another day has past at the river,
a chill in the air produces a shiver.
The wind pushes white caps,
on the shore they lap.

It's now evening time,
as I make these thoughts rhyme.
The sun sets in the west,
ready to put the day to rest.

Blue-gray clouds of phantom shape,
drift above the landscape.
Reminding of the trials in life,
those dark shadows causing strife.
Now Ghosts of the past,
a new life has been cast.

A ribbon of reddish-orange on water is cast,
in my memory this will last.
The ribbon shimmers with the waves,
the light dances like gems of crystals paved.

The sky turns to a pinkish hue;
Oh, what a delightful view.
The artistry of God's Work,
a prayer of thanks it provokes.

As the sun sets, I do a little yawning,
then wait for a new dawning.
There is a hush in the night,
Gods says, be still and know my might.

So it is with life's setting sun,
our soul shall dwell with the risen Son.
He promises a new dawning, without a fading sun.

RG

John 3:26 "He that believeth on the Son hath everlasting life." (John 3:47,KJ)

Written on a prison cell wall; "I believe in the sun, even whence it is not shinning. I believe in love, even when I don't feel it. I believe in God, even when He is silent" AU "O death, where is they sting ? O grave, where is they victory?" (1 Cor. 15:55,KJ)

DOES GOD REALLY CARE ?

The Bible tells of the good shepherd,
and that we are His flock.
For all humanity is a herd,
I will find you despite the size of the flock.

He knows our name and our pain,
when we have reason to complain.
He knows our face,
our identity He can trace.

He knows every born child,
on that thought dwell awhile.
I have written your name,
and will be with you in your land.
When to me you call,
I'll find you on the roll call.

Express your needs to me,
for I'll be with thee.
In me place your trust,
as through life you thrust.

In the mean time you must smile,
for I'll be along in a little while.

RG

PSALM 23

The Lord is my shepherd;
I shall not want.
He makes me to lie down in green pastures;
He leads me beside still waters.
He restores my soul:
He leads me in the paths of righteousness,
For His name's sake.

Yes, though I walk through the valley of
the shadow of death,
I will fear no evil;
for you are with me;
They rod and staff they comfort me.

Thou prepare a table before me in the
presence of my enemies;
You anoint my head with oil;
my cup runneth over.

Surely goodness and mercy shall follow me
all the days of my life;
And I will dwell in the house of the Lord forever.

GOD'S WHISPERING HOPE

The Holy Spirit is heaven's silent voice,
we hear it as our choice.
Listen to the whisper.

We become God's guest,
received at our request.
Listen to the whisper.

It touches our soul,
like winds gentle flow.
Listen to the whisper.

In solitude we hear the message,
recorded in the Good Book passage.
Listen to the whisper.

The whisper is an encompassing force,
for assurance reach for the source.
Listen to the whisper.

Daily through life we trod,
living by the grace of God.
Listen to the whisper.

God's whispering hope,
gives the faith to cope.
Listen to the "Whisper".

                                        RG

If we don't listen to God's whispering hope, then life is meaningless. And, if we don't believe that our soul is homeward bound, then faith is worthless and futile. Our purpose for living becomes a tragedy resulting in a dead end street, with Christ's promises being fruitless. It is our assignment and responsibility to draw attention to God's Word, which fulfills not only His precepts and promises, but the interpretation of hymns sung and poems read. These all reflect the workings of the indwelling spirit. In other words "Christ's work" regardless of our inability to capture the full meanings and significance of "The Wonder of it All". Christ brought with Him "God's Whispering Hope" for all humankind. God's whispering hope was evident at Pentecost. It came in like the wind. That wind (spirit) has blown throughout humanity for over two thousand years. Christ's birth and death on the cross gave us salvation for the remission of sins. It is a covenant and promise. All is guaranteed in God's Word.

Crossing The Bridge

Cross the bridge and set the course.
　　　　Follow the beacon form God's lighthouse.
A bridge to cross any day.
　　　　It won't waiver or sway.
Pass over the bridge.
　　　　Then your soul to God pledge.

CROSSING THE BRIDGE

All bridges have component parts,
its design is a special art.
Design precedes construction,
assuring its safe function.

The bridge of faith is the same,
now each element to name.
Assembled, it will carry our soul,
thus serving a special role.

Now identify with me if you will,
surely it will please God's Will.
The foundation is God,
is concrete like rock, reinforced with His rod.
Now the columns giving vertical support,
these to God we report.

The column of courage,
the inspiration through life to portage.
The column of prayer,
words to God to avoid being a stray.
The column of the grateful heart,
counting our blessings daily before we depart.
The column of peace,
glad tidings daily to release.
The column of hope,
gives us the strength to cope.

Horizontal beams spanning the posts,
out-stretched arms of the heavenly host.
Our faith is the deck of the bridge,
each support having God's tutelage.

All bridges are subjected to stress,
compression, tensile, inertia, elasticity and shear.

Life quickly reminds us of daily distress.
The bridge of faith is strong, do not fear,
Christ tells us ever so clear.

The spirit of God is the cementing agent,
binding a soul forever transient.
A bridge to cross any day,
it won't waiver or sway.

So cross the bridge of faith and set the course,
follow the beacon from God's house.
Steadfast journey toward the beacons source.
Destination, "Heavens Shore" to dwell in God's house.
Pass over the bridge,
then your soul to God pledge.

RG

HOMEWARD BOUND
By Roger Goodman

Now lend me your ears,
as now before God we appear.
A special persons deeds to hear,
words said fervently clear.

At his/her funeral, thank you for your attendance,
now present to honor in remembrance.
Farewell; Dear Husband, Dear Dad, Dear Grandpa
Dear Great Grandpa, Dear Friend.

To you this message we send.
Your life on earth is at an end,
your love and gracious heart we came to depend.
Our gratitude we now extend,
as these thoughts are penned.

Though from our presence you depart,
fond memories dwell in our heart.
We shall miss your embrace,
visions in review we quickly trace.

Sorrow fills us with sweeping emotion,
in quietude, don't forget God's transformation.
Our prayers to heaven transcend,
humbly seeking God, our souls to mend.

We know you stand on heavens shore,
your departure we shan't deplore,
In God's scheme, death is planned,
otherwise how could we beside Him stand ?

Give us the wisdom to understand,
and the strength to withstand.
Dearest friend, we say farewell,
knowing it is God's Will.

Knowing that you are on heavens shore holding God's
hand,
through Christ's salvation there is a promised land.
God gave you life for a while,
now return it with a smile.

God's love all encompassing,
to give us a new dawning.
Today we say good-bye with sorrow,
knowing that we'll join you tomorrow.

THE PASSING BELL TOLLS
By Roger A. Goodman

Today the passing bell tolls for me,
tomorrow it will ring for thee.
God summons with His beckoning call,
life's earthly end, life's closure for all.

Dear God, I know You're in control,
forgive the trembling in my soul,
In you I entrust my life,
yet, I struggle in this moment of strife.

Though this moment draws near,
to the future I must peer.
Should I tremble with great fear ?
Then I remember, Christ's message ever so clear.

Jesus said, "I'll never forsake thee".
He sheds light on the valley of death for me.
He leadth me so that I can see,
along the pathway to eternity.

He bids all the darkness to flee,
my savior has come to me.
He carries me over the abyss,
my soul He fills with bliss.

He cleansed my sins, in my stead,
clearing the path for me to tread.
Now I shall see Him face to face,
to thank Him for His saving grace.
"Just As I Am", I gladly sing the song,
my praises to Jesus belong.
There I shall find restful peace,
my faith, His love shall never cease.

Let the church bells ring,
join the chimes with joyful sing.
Sing with rejoicing voices,
those hymns of special choices.

When Christ came into this world, there was rejoicing.
When Christ lived, there was rejoicing.
When Christ died, there was rejoicing,
In Christ's honor, at my passing, let there be rejoicing.

My passing bell tolls,
my name shall appear on God's scroll.
God gave me life for awhile,
now I return it with a smile.

A smile to show appreciation;
For His creation.
For my life's duration.
For His redemption.
For His salvation.
For eternal life, "My Continuation."

ON HEAVENS SHORE
By Roger A. Goodman

Time to cross the bridge of faith and set the course,
now to follow the beacon from God's house.
Time to steadfast journey to the beacons source,
destination, "Heavens Shore" to dwell in God's house.
Time to pass over the bridge,
then my soul to God pledge.

Yet, my soul cryeth out, but no one hears,
eternal darkness, what a dreadful fear.
But wait, there's a light on the distant shore,
God's beacon, a bearing, a direction to soar.

He shall hear my humble cry,
and not pass me by.
The strength of His spirit shall prevail,
as on this journey I set sail.
My faith in Him shall not fail,
although, now my body is frail.

Though my departure is sad,
His beacon of light makes me glad.
Yes, He is calling me today,
it is time to go without delay.

Though I forfeit earthly treasure,
I accept God's Will in fullest measure.
My faith is His spirit of power,
which grows in this darkest hour.

I will see the works of the almighty,
on heavens shore when I land.
Tis His communion I find,
what a triumph this will bring.
Evermore a reason to sing,
let the hymns rise with a joyful ring.

The distant shore has a firm foundation,
wrought with Christ's salvation.
I have a new divine,
I say to the Lord, "I Am Thine".

His glory on the pathway doth shine,
His beacon set the voyage just fine.
There's a cheer in this heart of mine,
to the pinnacle of my faith, I did climb.
Once the darkness of this night is past,
the morning on heavens shore shall break at last.
There to dwell in my heavenly home,
eternal peace, free to roam.
Safely arriving on heavens shore,
now to dwell for evermore.

A freedom of blessed liberty,
Christ's promise now a reality.
A grand reward for Christianity,
graciously received for eternity.
My soul to my body He restoreth,
a new life in heaven, now I must goeth.

It fills my soul with wonder,
as this voyage I ponder.
Looking to the distant shore yonder.
He leadeth the way, I shan't flounder.
I close my life on this final voyage,
ending life's long search for this passage.

My life's searching finally found,
on heavens shore safe and sound.
Peace, joy, goodwill shall abound,
I shall rejoice with great resound.
There I shall rise each moring,
in awe of this new dawning.
From worldly woes I am set free,
filling my heart with glee.

Though my body in grave lay still,
God's voice whispers His will.
Shall my journey be in vain ?
He is the link in the eternal chain.
He shall receive me just as I am,
His pardon, to which I say "Amen".
His pardon I shall receive,
this I have reason to believe.

To those I leave behind,
it brings clouds of sorrow.
Look to the Lord and you'll find,
strength for tomorrow.
Remember, tomorrow I will greet you on heavens shore,
there, together, we shall roam for evermore.

DEATH IS PART OF GOD'S PLAN

God gave us life.
Yet, we experience death and strife.
Is His plan unfair?
Sometimes we think this in despair.

God promises to take care of us in sickness and health,
for in his faithfulness there is great wealth.
God in His grace he gave us a spirit,
to behold as a given right.

A right to make a choice,
to accept salvation and rejoice.
Thus death can be traded in for life eternal,
earthly life gives way to the immortal.

With Christ at our side we make the journey,
faith in his spirit makes it a certainty.
Yes, we were born to die,
Yet, in heaven we shall lie.

Oh, "The Wonder of it All."
When we hear his beckoning call.
We shall not travel alone,
He will join us, so don't be forlorn.

As Christ was risen,
we shall, too, arise.

RG

LIFE CAN BE FOREVER

Imagine earthly life,
plus everlasting life.
A journey where we can forever roam,
for Christ promised a heavenly room.

On the cross he performed his task,
so that we could in his grace bask.
Though we are subject to sinful ways,
we'll shed those stains on that glorious day.

A faith dream come true,
a rebirth and life anew.
We shall awake to a wondrous view,
In the Bible he has given us precious clues.

A dawning like a baby's first breathe,
to witness first hand heaven breadth.
All because Christ loves us,
only if in him we trust.

RG

GATEWAY TO HEAVEN

Only through Jesus do we enter God's domain,
His grace makes it possible to with him reign.

Our savior stands at the gate,
with his approval we enter without debate.

Through salvation there is a blessed assurance,
by the wave of his hand we make the entrance.

The greatest gift ever, to live forever.

RG

HYMN: GREAT IS THY FAITHFULNESS

Great is thy faithfulness,
O God, my Father;
There is no shadow of turning with Thee,
Thou changest not;
Thy compassions, they fail not.
As Thou hast been,
Thou forever wilt be.

Summer and winter,
and spring time and harvest,
sun, moon, stars in their courses above,
Join with all nature in manifold witness,
to they great faithfulness, mercy and love.

Pardon for sin and a peace that endureth,
They own dear presence to cheer and to guide.
Strength for today and bright hope for tomorrow,
blessings all mine with ten thousand besides.
Great is they faithfulness.

Words; Thomas O. Chislom
Music: William M. Runyan
C 1923, Red. 1951 Hope Publishing Company
Carol Stream, IL 60188
All rights reserved. Used by permission.
Reprinted under license #65475

NEARER, MY GOD. TO THEE

Nearer my God to Thee,
    nearer to Thee.
Even thought it be a cross,
    that raiseth me !
Still all my song shall be,
    nearer my God to thee.

Then, with my waking thoughts,
    bright with Thy praise.
Out of my stony grief,
    Bethel, I'll raise;
So be my woes to Thee,
    nearer my God to Thee.

Or if, on joyful wing,
    cleaving the sky.
Sun, moon and stars forgot,
    up-ward I fly.
Still all my song shall be,
    nearer my God to Thee.

The Celebration Hymnal

HYMN: COME, THOU FOUNT OF EVERY BLESSING

Come, Thou fount of every blessing,
Tune my heart to sing Thy grace;
Streams of mercies, never ceasing.
Call for songs of loudest praise.
Teach me some melodious sonnet,
Sung by flaming tongues above;
Prasie His name, I'm fixed upon it,
Name of God's redeeming love.

Hither to Thy love has blest me;
Thou hast brought me to this place;
And I know Thy hand will bring me
Jesus sought me when a stranger,
Wandering from the fold of God;
He, to rescue me from danger,
Brought me with His precious blood.

O to grace how great a debtor or
daily I'm constrained to be !
Let thy goodness like a fetter,
Bind my wandering heart to Thee;
Prone to wander, Lord I feel it,
Prone to leave the God I love;
Here's my heart, O take and seal it;
Seal it for Thy courts above.

The Celebration Hymnal

AS A MAN THINKETH

Psalm 105:1-6 "Oh, give thanks to the Lord ! Call upon
His name; make know His deeds among the peoples !
Sing to Him, sing psalms to Him; talk of all His wondrous
Works ! Glory in His holy name; Let the hearts of those
who seek the Lord ! Seek the Lord and His strength;
Seek His face evermore ! Remember His marvelous works
which He has done. His wonders, and the judgements of
His mouth.

CHAPTER 14:

AS A MAN THINKETH

Philippians 1:27 "Only let your conduct be worthy of the gospel of Christ, so that whether I come and see you or am absent, I may hear of your affairs, That you stand fast in one spirit with one mind striving together for the faith of the gospel.

When living in Christ it is the seeking that kindles the spiritual flame. God has put in our imagination countless treasures. The discoveries are the ambers that make our faith grow and glow. Shinning so that others my know. To know Christ and to make Christ known.

God has endowed in each of us diversified gifts. Offering what we have to serve Christ is our purpose in life. In doing so, amazing things can and do happen. The contents of this book testify to that conclusion. God is a diversified God. His diversity shows up in our image, therefore, through us He displays His creative genius. The thoughts, words or works of the hands have been done in "Remembrance of our Savior". For without him, this endeavor would have been fruitless and meaningless. The power of Christ's spirit in human beings can and do over-come great obstacles in life. It is the grace of God at work in all of us. It is an invisible and endless stream that fills our soul and guides us along life's journey.

JESUS IN OUR WORKS

Is Jesus involved in our works ? Most certainly he is, for we are his workmanship. Our faith gives us the motivation to do good deeds and share our gifts. I recall with unpleasant recollection a statement made by a minister delivering a message from the lectern during a Sunday morning worship service. His comment was "....such works show that we are insufficient in Christ. Such works are not worthy of acknowledgment, for they deliver the wrong message." Essentially pooh-poohing innovative ways to draw attention to our Lord. If it were not for the innovation of Christians, churches would have not been built or write the curriculum to teach the ways of Christianity. Perhaps ministers should more readily realize that they don't govern the Holy Spirit. It is beyond our comprehension and most certainly out of our domain to control. For we must remember Emmanuel; "God is with us". He is everywhere all at the same time. I surmise that some people put a fence around the Bible. When we open the pages of God's Word the spirit should be allowed to flow freely for all to grasp the Kingdom of God. For He is the wind that blows constantly touching the heart beat of humanity. If we tune into that spirit, remarkable things can and do happen. To some degree it has captivated me. He touches all creatures big and small, the little and the big thinkers as well as gifts big and small. Such works afford us the opportunity to explore God's identity and ours as well. It is the searching that opens the mind and the heart to the sanctity of life and all that God is. The Bible tells us to let our hearts guide us. "Let us consider one another in order to stir up love and do good works." (Heb. 10:24 IBML) God has provided us with abundant gifts. We are privileged to untie the ribbon. When we untie the ribbon the treasures of "The Wonder of it all" are revealed.

Some Pastors have the mind set that such works are a Jesus plus attitude, in other words Jesus is insufficient in our lives. There is much we can add to the statement "Jesus plus". Jesus plus worship. Jesus plus praise. Jesus plus manifestation of the spirit. Jesus plus our works. Jesus plus our attitude and Jesus plus our love. Yes, Jesus is adequate for our salvation, however, he asks for much more. For we are Jesus plus. The plus is to make Jesus known by how his spirit influences us. Yes, it is a Jesus plus situation. For there are two forces in play in our Christian lives. That being God's Creative Genius and Christ's redemptive grace. One can not exist without the other. As a matter of fact God's Creative Genius came first. For which we express our gratitude each morning when we arise. Christ is sufficient for our salvation. However, our works are necessary to draw attention to the grace of our Lord. God has endowed each of us with spiritual as well as personal abilities to accomplish that God given assignment. Being adopted as sons/daughters of God through Jesus Christ gives us the privilege to help magnify the wonder of His work. There is only one way that can be accomplished. And, that is through us and the church. For whosoever beholds the Kingdom has the duty to spread the word. "In all your ways acknowledge Him, and He shall direct your path." (Prov. 3:5, IBML) in doing so, He wants us to be filled with the spirit in our doings and our goings. "And God can give more blessings than we need. Then you will always have plenty to give to others". (2 Cor. 9:8, KJ) To a great degree I have incorporated into my writings words spoken by Jesus and his disciples. By these works I do not place myself higher on the cross. Regardless of our position in life we all stand at the base of the cross equally ashamed. What I do offer is a collection of thoughts in the form of poems and deeds of the hands to proclaim my interest in "The Wonder of it all". The merits of its worthiness, acceptability and approval is subject to justification by the Holy Spirit and the critique of readers. The silent mind is wasteful to the soul and to others. Poems and works of the hands can be and is a form of ministry. The mind imagines scripture and the hands are an extension by words and works. Without it we would be of little use to God's mission. Can you imagine what life would be like without it ? Failures, in deed. Hymn "Lift Your Hearts, Raise Your Voice". I would amend that by saying, "Lift up your works". For we are God's investment. People will know us as Christians through the testimony of our works. Such works do not circumvent the fact that "The Lord is my sheppard", not my pen or the fabrication of things by my hands. For God is the wondrous one and we all are the benefactors of "The Wonder of it all". This is true not only in the present, but in the here-after as well. How great the glory of God's wonderful things. By birthright we have the distinct privelege to have access to God's gifts. Behold, the wonders of works.

It is the taping into His wonders that gives life purpose and meaning. Is it right to ask God to bless my works? " Absolutely, ask and it will be given to you. That philosophy under girds our relationship with our Lord. "Yet, ye have not, because ye ask not." (James 4:2, KJ)

When all is said and done it comes down to "What a Man Thinketh." Especially as it pertains to how we behold "The Wonder of it All." "Be a worker who is not ashamed and who uses the true teaching in the right way". (2 Tim 2:15, KJ) All of us are seeking God's blessings. When it is answered, we more thoroughly come to realize the hand of God in our affairs. New ambitions are born and nurtured by the spirit. It propels us forward to accomplish worthy tasks. We feel more alive and in tune with our maker and inspector. Behold "The Wonders of Inspiration". Jesus said "Unless you see signs and wonders you will in no way believe." (John 4:48, KJ) Hopefully, this has been reflected and demonstrated by my writings and my hands. Often when we are concentrating on our works it affords us the opportunity to grasp the meaning and depth of God's creative genius and grace in us. We begin to more readily internalize the blessings of our gifts. Through our works we witness the invisible at work. "Therefore, we do not lose heart, even though our outward man is perishing, yet the inward man is being renewed day by day." (2 Cor, 4:16, KJ) As we show forth our faith it is unveiled in our gifted works. Although what we see is temporary, it does help prepare our heart, mind and soul for the future journey ahead. For there is a correlation between faith and works. God wants us to learn from each other. For we are His workmanship.

THE REASONS

When approaching a significant task such as these works in the name of the Lord, Jesus Christ, a person must be mindful of its justification. Therefore, these scriptural passages provide the incentive to proceed, not in self-rightousness, but in faith.

"Let everthing that has breath praise the Lord !" (Psalm 150:2, KJ)

"Praise Him for His mighty acts. Praise Him according to His excellent greatness." (Psalm 150:2, KJ)

"Let each one give as he purposes in his heart, not grudgingly or of necessity, for God loves the cheerful giver." (2 Cor. 9:8, D3ML)

"O Lord, You are my God; I will exalt thee, I will praise thy name, for thou hast done wonderful things...." (Isiah 25:1, KJ)

"Many, O Lord, my God, are thy wonderful works which hast done; and you thoughts toward us....they are more than can be numbered." (Psalm 40:5, IBML)

"If there is anything praise worthy, think on these things." (Phil. 4:8, KJ)

"Neglect not the gift that is in you." (1 Tim. 4:14, KJ)

"Having then gifts differing according to the grace that is given us, let us use them...." (Rom. 12:6, KJ)

"Whatever your hand finds to do, do it with all your might." (Ecc. 9:10, IBML)

"He who has a slack hand becomes poor, but the hand of the diligent makes one rich." (Prov. 10:4, IBML)

"For we are His workmanship created in Christ Jesus for good Works." (Eph. 2:10, KJ)"Be confident of this very thing, that God has begun a good work in you and will complete it...." (Phil. 1:6, KJ)

Isiah 50:9 "Surely the Lord God will help me." (Isiah 50:9, IBML)

THE DOINGS

"Can you search out the deep things of God ? Can you find out the limits of the Almighty ? They are higher than the heavens." (Job. 11:7,8 IBML)

"Oh, give thanks to the Lord, for He is so good ! His loving kindness is forever." (Psalm 118:1, KJ)

"Be renewed in the spirit of the mind." (Eph. 4:23, KJ)

"And I will give you a new heart and put a new spirit within you." (Ezek. 36:26, IBML)

"All shall speak of the might of Your awesome acts and I will declare Your greatness." (Psalm 145:6, IBML)

"And the Lord shall make thee plenteous in goods, in the fruit of they body." (Deut. 28:11, KJ)
"And let us consider one another to provoke unto love and to good works." (Heb. 10:24, KJ)

"A dream comes through much activity." (Ecc. 5:3, IBML)

"You shall be like a tree planted by the river water, that brings forth its fruit in its season, whose leaf shall not wither, and whatever you do shall prosper." (Psalm 1:3, KJ)

" If you sow sparingly you will reap sparingly. If you who sow bountifully you will also reap bountifully." (2 Cor. 9:6, KJ)

"Happy is the man that findeth wisdom, and the man that getteth understanding." (Prov. 3:13, KJ)

"As a Christian you can be a preacher of the gospel and share the good news of salvation with family, friends and neighbors." (Mark 16:15, KJ)

"For God hath not given us the spirit of fear; but of power, and of love, And of a sound mind." (2 Tim. 1:7, KJ)

"Stand fast therefore in the liberty by which Christ has made us free. Freedom has made possible this book. (Gal. 5:1, KJ)

"Do you see that faith works together with works, and by works faith is made perfect."(James 2:22, E3ML)

"If you have faith as a mustard seed, you say to this mountian move.... and it will move and nothing will be impossible for you." Matt. 17:20, KJ)

"Lift up your eyes on high, and behold who hath created these things, that bringeth out their host by numbers; he calleth them all by name and the Greatness of His might, for that he is strong in power; not one faileth." (Isiah 40:26, KJ)

Mark 9:23 "All things are possible to them that beleive." (Mark 9:23, KJ)

1 Thessalonians 5:18 "In everything give thanks, for this is the Will of God in Christ Jesus for us."(I Thess. 5:18, IBML)

Note: Our lives have a great worth when you use it to minister to the needs of others; telling them about the good news of salvation through Jesus Christ and about his love and kindess".

Note: The cover of this book shows an eagle soaring above a valley. The wind gives him flight and takes him where he wants to go. He is free. Like the eagle we are free to praise the Lord.

SHARING OUR WORKS

"....a workman that needeth not be ashamed,
rightly dividing the word of truth."

Our works can and do help us to place one step after the other in our journey through life. God's word tells us to be steadfast and bold in our Christian faith. In other words, be not afraid to display the convictions in our hearts. It is that motivation that stirs the desire that propels us forward to accomplish our works to cheer other people onward toward that ultimate goal and glorious day. "Let us consider one another in order to stir up love and good works, not forsaking the assembling of ourselves together, as is the manner of some, but exhorting one another, and so much the more as you see the day approaching" (Heb. 10:24, KJ) Our Lord expects us to fulfill that assignment. But we must be cautious in our works. For the Lord said "For by grace you have been saved through faith, and not of yourselves, it is the gift of God not of works, least anyone should boast. For we are his workmanship, created in Christ Jesus for good works, which God prepared before hand that we should walk in them." It should be emphasized that our good works are an extension of our faith expressed by voice, writing or crafty hands. The hands, especially, are an extension of mind, heart and soul. Some people live by the misconception that I will do a lot of good deeds, therefore, I will be guaranteed my entrance to heaven. However, that is not the case. God will not look upon deeds done for personal magnification, pride, glory or the expectation of a heavenly reward is not the objective. If that were true, then countless sinners would be let through the gates of heaven. Heaven is not a haven but a gift. We have to remember that Christ holds in his hands the roster of names of people who are worthy when the roll is announced. That is not the reason that God granted each of us special abilities. It behooves each one of us to utilize our God ordained skills according God's wishes. For He is the Master Conductor of life's concert and symphony of all things. Such knowledge prompts us to help build good faith in the eyes of our maker. It is an assigned expectation. As matter of fact it is a commandment "Love thy neighbor as you love your self." Out of love for one another we do good works for one another and He will be the final judge, not us. The commandment explicitly defines our role as Christian's. Interpreted, that means to practice the "Golden Rule". Do unto others as you would have them do unto you. "But the fruit of the spirit is love, joy...." (Gal.5:22, KJ) The fruit of the spirit is our spirit at work. The spirit provides the desire, inspiration, and willingness to share our good deeds. By sharing our talents we bring gladness and good tidings to the people around us. It is the Holy Spirit at work in us. The Great Commission tells us that is our assignment and responsibility. Commandment: "Love thy God with all your mind, heart and soul." "Let your light so shine before men, that they may see your good works, and glorify your Father which is in heaven." (Matt. 5:16, KJ) Least we forget our gifted deeds. "Remembering without ceasing your work of faith, and labor of love." (Thess. 1:3) For it is the love for our fellow person that we put forth our works. In our brotherly/sisterly relationship in Christ we are obligated not only to nurture and sustain that principle of living, but to fortify it with good works. Our reputation is known by our works and words. We will be judged by our good works and the redemptive grace of our Lord, Jesus Christ. It is not our works, rather it is the grace we display in the image of our Lord. It is an honor to dwell, live, and do good works in that image where we acknowledge, recognize, and accept the Father, the Son and the Holy Spirit. What works in the spirit, lives in the spirit. Through us it serves as a continuous burning flame. Our Lord ignites and kindles the flame. We receive and we give according to God's gift in us. Otherwise our works become meaningless and worthless. We love our children, family and friends enough to do good deeds for them. Because of God's creative genius in us how much more we should pay tribute to our maker. For because of that gift we have the ability as well as the privilege to accomplish good works in His name. It is because of him that we are granted the freedom and permission to use his name in our works. It is grace that perpetuates our philosophy and willingness to offer our good works to humankind. For by grace it exists. Paul said in (Colossians 2:2, KJ) ". . . and attaining to all riches in full assurance of understanding to the knowledge of the mystery of God, both the Father and of Christ in whom are hidden all the treasures of wisdom and knowledge." "....since the day we heard it, do not cease to pray for you, and to ask that you may be filled with the knowledge of His will in all wisdom and spiritual understanding, that you may walk worthy of the Lord, fully pleasing Him, being fruitful in every good work and increasing in the knowledge of God." (Col. 1:9-10, KJ) As we journey along the pathway of "The wonder of it All" we many times discover our spiritual abilities as it applies to our purpose in life. God speaks to us in unusual ways. Knowledge of Him inspires our works such as writing a hymn or a poem, writing a book or design a stained glass piece of work that serves as a vehicle for artistic expression.

Because God is invisible there is a great need to fold into our works innovative ways to draw attention to the creative genius, the power, the grace, and the magnitude of His presence in our daily lives. Because the Spirit of Christ is a ghostly figure, we turn to our earthly natural inborn traits and skills to simulate, to symbolize or to fabricate ways to better comprehend the nature of our creator. By analogy we can interpret God and determine how He is so magnificently infused and manifested the spirit into our character. God breathed into us the capacity to comprehend and apply our learning's. By His grace we become His workmanship. In our personage we do not stand alone. Jesus said "Never will I leave you; never will I forsake you!" "By Him, therefore, let us offer the sacrifice of praise to God continually, that is, the fruit of our lips giving thanks to his name. But to do good and to communicate forget not: for with such sacrifices God is well pleased."(Heb. 13:5, KJ) The Lord is with us every moment we spend applying our gifts. He helps to fortify and carry us when we undertake a Christian assignment and stays with us to the very end. Then He applauds us and praises us for doing good. "Trust in the Lord, and be good....and He shall give us the desires of our hearts." (Psalm 4:13, KJ) Many times the voice of our Lord speaks and initiates us, therefore, compelling us to do good works by releasing the gift that harbors in our conscience. When we are working on our Christian assignments we more clearly hear His voice and listen to "God's Whispering Hope." "I can do all things through Christ which strengthened me." (Phil.4:13, KJ) If we let the spirit and the image of Christ dwell in our hearts we discover the reason for accomplishing good works. It helps us to mold the purpose for singing, writing, designing or fabricating good works. "For we are God's fellow workers; you are God's field, God's building...

so then, men ought to regard us as servants of Christ and as those entrusted with the secret things of God." (1 Cor. 3:9,IBML) What a high honor we receive when He entrusts us with His image, His Spirit, His works, His proclamations and His blessings to be a disciple of the Son of God. What a privilege it is to make that choice in life. "Now then, we are ambassadors of Christ, as though God were appealing through us; we employ you on Christ's behalf, be reconciled to God." (2 Cor. 5:20, IBML) That becomes a pledge to the message of God. That is precisely why God created man/woman with such a diversity of skills. Skills that when mixed together satisfies God's Master Plan. "Having gifts that differ according to the grace given us, let us use them." (Rom.12:6, IBML) "There are diversities of gifts, but the same spirit....But one and same works all these things, distributing to each one individually as He wills."(1 Cor. 12:4, KJ) "Do not neglect the gift that is in you, which was given by prophecy...." (1 Tim. 4:14, KJ)

When we do good works for the Lord that benefits others it manifests itself in our works. "By their fruits ye shall know them." (Matt.7:20, IBML) Our good works bears the fruits of labor. It is God's Will that we mesh into our being individual talents to help deliver His message to humankind. The future generations depend on it. "But the manifestation of the Spirit is given to each for the profit of all: for to one is given the word of wisdom through the Spirit, to another the word of knowledge through the same Spirit....But one and the same Spirit works all these things, distributing to each individually as He will." (1 Cor. 12:7, IBML) "And we all know that all things work together for the good to those who love God, to those who are called to His purpose." (Rom.8:28, KJ) "That you may walk worthy of the Lord, fully pleasing Him, being fruitful in every good works and increasing in the knowledge of God." (Col.1: 10, KJ) "....be filled with the knowledge of His Will....and spiritual understanding." (Col.1:9,KJ)

It is right and our duty is to share our innate abilities. For Prov. 17:8, KJ, tells us "A gift is as a precious stone in the eyes of him that hath it: whether so ever it turneth, it prospereth." "And also that every man/woman should eat and drink, and enjoy the good of their labor, it is the gift of God." (Ecc. 3:13,KJ) There is great joy and freedom of spirit found in applying our natural talents whether it be writing hymns, poetry, books or a display of our artistic expression. For through those works we are afforded the opportunity to communicate with other prople on this planet. Religious artistic works have been used extensively through out the history of the church as well as in Christian books to help convey the precepts of Christendom. They help to fortify the message of our Lord and Savior. How unforunate it would be to dismiss the value of such works in the history of the spirit working through our endeavors. This scriptural reading states and confirms that statement. "Neglect not the gift that is in thee...." (1 Tim.4:14,KJ) There is a twofold implication when interpreting that passage. Of course, the primary understanding is that it is the gift of the image and Spirit of Christ within us. Gifts born to us through salvation. We are asked to function within the parameters of that image as a partner to our creator. Most importantly, that the Godly ordained gift in us is to be disciples to bring glory to His name and to assist bringing potential candidates to the awareness of salvation. The discipline to write, sing, to lead others and the capability to use artistic skills to help spread the message of our Lord inherent to that belief. God is a God of great variety, therefore, there is great diversity throughout humanity for very specific reasons. It is interesting how He works through us. For without us the influence of our Lord would be greatly diminished. We are significant soldiers marching forward in the glory of His name.

Throughout the remaining portion of this chapter numerous scripture readings are referenced. To some degree these passages have been randomly selected. It will appear mundane, however, there is a reason and a purpose for including many more Bible readings. Primarily it is to magnify the significance that our Lord puts our faith in action through our Christian works. In addition, to emphasize the great need and importance of serving our leader of the human race. We should not only take from the Lord, but to continue contributing our fare share. His grace is our grace and we should respond accordingly with generosity, our caring and our worthiness as a Christian. Some people would claim that works done in the name of our Lord is in vain and not significant to the Kingdom of God. We are in deed a member of

His Kingdom as practicing Christians, for He created us to do good works for the benefit of His children on earth. We don't do it to expect or earn eternal life. Such motives would display arrogrance and a lack of humility. However, it is integral to that qualification. For we are His children here to demonstrate our works that are inspired by the Spirit of Christ as seen in the image of God himself. We were made in the image of God. Therefore, we paint our image as a person. It shows people around us that we are Christians. It displays how we were designed by God himself. Of course, due to the nature of humankind modifications to our attitude and conduct is necessary to fulfill the expectations of our purpose on earth.

He is in constant surveillance as to whether or not we do good deeds by walking in his image. Our performance will be tested and evaluated accordingly as we approach that ultimate judgement day. Yes, there shall be a reward for doing good works. It is part of our faith and belief. "My children let us not love in word or in tongue, but in deed and in truth." (1 John 3:18, KJ) Good works are out actions seen through our steadfast faith. "Search me, O God, and know my heart." (Psalm 139:23, KJ) Our good works reveals our spirit that fosters and magnifies such deeds. Remembering that He is capable of reading our motives for producing such deeds. It is a measure of our grace. By way of God's grace inherent to our gifts and purpose in life, He has granted us an entitlement. That entitlement gives us the freedom to discover and put into practice unique ways to draw attention to our creator. "Walk worthy of the vocation where with you are called." (Eph. 4:1, KJ) Each of us have a calling to contribute to the Christian movement in our culture. Pastor's, Minister's, or Priest's lead, but we play the role in the movie of life. "For all things there is a season." Thus experiencing new dimensions and avenues to pursue as well as performing our responsibilities. We become the blooming flower in God's field for others to see. Our expressions go on display in God's gallery for other to unveil. Thus reaping the benefits and the harvest of "The Wonder of it All." Through our works we plant the seed of insight, encouragement and hope. "And we desire that each one of you show the same diligence to the full assurance of hope until the end; that you do not become sluggish." (Heb. 6:11, IBML) That is our Lord cheering us on. It means that we never give up our abilities as practicing Christian's. We are charged with the responsibility to discover our gifts and improve our performance in those areas where we can best fit into the scheme of Christendom. Our talents should be fine tuned to the best of our ability. It helps to ascertain and measure our confidence in ourselves as well as our faith. We received the gift, therefore, we should weave it into our habits. In doing so, it is a reciprocal by showing God our appreciation for having been given such a privilege. For we are God's creation. "A good man out of the good treasures of his heart bringeth forth good things." (Matt. 12:35, KJ) For many people their God given abilities lay dormant. They sit idle lacking the inspiration, willingness and courage to reveal their gift to other people. They lack the initiative or deisire to fertilize their creative seed and bring it to the attention of our creator. They have not captured the full meaning of God's gift and expectations planted in them. "And let us not grow weary while doing good, for in due season we shall reap if we faint not. Therefore, as we have opportunity let us do good to all, especially to those who are of the household of faith." (Gal. 6:9. KJ)

As a teacher I never ceased to be amazed at the influence our works had on future generations. We transfer our insights whether it be by voice or by our hands. God smiles on our honest accomplishments, for He knows how it paves the road for the generations to come. God bestowed that privilege, opportunity, and responsibility so that good works through our willingness to have purpose and meaning inherent not only for earthly survival, but spiritual survival as well.".......But now you also must complete the doing of it; that as there was a readiness to desire it, so there may be a completion out of what you have. For there is a willing mind, it is accepted to what one has, and not according to what he does not have." (2 Cor. 8:12, IBML) By the spirit when we are ready the Lord working through us infuses in us the willingness to make contributions via talents for the benefit of people around us and the glory of the divine one who created the gift in us. Such giving is a matter of generosity, not of obligation. For we work in the glory of our Lord, then our deeds are worthy of acknowledgement and recognition. For the Lord praises those who give with a cheerful heart. He cheers on the cheerful giver. "He who sows sparingly will reap sparingly, and he who sows bountifully will also reap bountifully. So let each one give as he purposes in his heart.....And God is able to make all grace abound toward you, that you, always having self-sufficiency in all things may have abundance of every good works." (2 Cor. 9:8, KJ) "But he who glories, let him glory in the Lord." (2 Cor. 10:17, KJ) Our works define our character and commitment to Christianity. "You have not because you ask not." (James 4:2, KJ) Don't be afraid to pray to the Master Teacher to help you discover your God ordained gifts. This requires honesty and integrity in self-examination. For hidden within each of us are potential hidden secrets. Ask God to bless them, it will help to reveal those hidden talents. "For God hath not given us the spirit of fear; but of power, and of love, and of a sound mind." (2 Tim. 1:7, KJ) There is power in good deeds. It can and will influence other people. It draws attention to the magnificent gift inborn to us in manifold ways. "Finally, brethen, whatsoever things are of good report, if there be any virtue, and if there be any praise, think on these things." (Phil.4:8, KJ) As this applies to doing good works, whatsoever is genuine in purpose and intent should guide our motivations for having accomplished such deeds. Paul said "Rejoice in the Lord always, again I say, rejoice" (Phil. 4:14, KJ) We can rejoice in our good works because it is for the benefit and betterment of God's children. For we know that he rejoices with us. "Even so every good tree bringeth forth good Fruit...." (Matt. 7:17, KJ) "Wherefore by their fruits ye shall know them: (Matt. 7:20,KJ) "....but he that doeth the will of my Father which is in heaven." (Matt. 7:21, KJ) Whenever we go on a mission to do good work we first must start by asking ourselves "Will our works meet the expectations and worthiness of the Master of all things?"Any thing done for self-righteousness is wrong. It will fall on the deaf ears of our Lord. Any works done to spiritually elevate themselves above others is self-centeredness, useless and not worthy in the eyes of our Lord. Any works done to satisfy God's Will is valid. Any works to enhance and promote Christianity is worthy of the gracious heart of our Father in heaven. Any works to rescue a lost soul is praiseworthy. Whatever is good works for the benefit of all in the spirit of Christianity is worthy for other people to witness and observe. The final judgment is in the hands of the Lord Almightly. It is to Him that we surrender our good deeds. "Be steadfast, immovable, always abounding in the work of the Lord,...." (1Cor. 15:58,KJ)

As we go about our good works He recognizes and acknowledges our willingness to accomplish good deeds for the present generations as well as future generations." And we all know that all things work together for good of those who love God, to those who are called to His purpose." (Rom.8:28, KJ) "For the Son of man shall come in the glory of His Father, His angels: and then He shall reward every man according to his works." (Matt. 16:27, KJ) So this is the key answer to the question "Are our works worthy in the sight of God?" Are our works relevant to salvation? Are our works on earth a pathway to eternity? Apparently there is a linkage between the two. If it be true that we are to some degree judged by our works, then it can be concluded that such endeavors are worthy and is an integral part of the redemptive grace of our Lord. Otherwise, such works would be declared as senseless by the God Head of all things. Works can and do display our acts of repentance. For we know that if our works shine for the Lord, his light shines on us as the keeper of His faith in us. For He has entrusted to us works for good deeds and the welfare of His children. He has the priority to examine our works as well as the desire, the inspiration and the motivation to put our efforts into the bank or treasury of God's Kingdom. They become our investments for judgment. He becomes the evaluator and it is He alone who registers our rating of good productivity. However, whether little or big the offering, he is the final judge. "....in sincerity of heart, as to Christ; not with eye service, as man pleases, but as a bond servant of Christ, doing the will of God from the heart, with goodwill doing service, as to the Lord, and not to men, knowing that whatever good anyone does, he will receive the same from the Lord " (Eph.6:6, KJ) "and this I pray, that your love may abound still more the things that are excellent, that you may be sincere and without offense till the day of Christ, be filled with the fruits of righteousness which are by Jesus Christ, to the glory and praise of God." (Phil. 1:9, KJ)

May the reader of this collection of thoughts presented in this book be worthy for consideration in their journey through life.

May it provide hope and encouragement as they steadfastly walk into the future. May the visions instilled and give insight to the image of Christ's benevolence and grace. This is my story of "The wonder of it all" as seen by my journey with the creator of all things, the leader of the human race. "And God is able to make all grace abound toward you, that you, always having all sufficiency in all things, may have an abundance for every good work." (2 Cor. 9:8, KJ) If this is truly internalized then we should discover that we have more blessings than we need. Therefore, with a gracious heart share it with others. As each of us discover the magnitude of our abilities we come to realize that God's work is infinite. If we do not use our good works, then it is wasted. We live once and have only one opportunity to incorporate it into our Christian walk. God's endowment of gifts in us doesn't come to frutition to assist God in His Master Plan. The silent mind and inactive hands are wasteful to the soul. "Share with God's people who are in need" (Rom. 12:13,KJ) "Many, O Lord, my God, are thy wonderful works which thou hast done; and your thoughts toward us they are more than can be numbered." (Psalm 40:5, KJ) "And I am sure that God who began the good work with in you will keep on helping you grow in His grace until His task with in you is finished." (Rom, 12:13,KJ) We would be remiss not to give God the credit for our gifted ways of assisting other people. For without Him we would not exist. Therefore, we would not be on assignment to deliver the message. He wants through our works "A cheerful heart doeth good like medicine" (Prov. 17:22, KJ) As we do good works our hearts abound with gladness for having the opportunity to touch another persons well being. That is what makes us brothers/sisters in the spirit. Why should we neglect sharing the treasures of our works? 'For we are His workmanship created in Christ Jesus unto good works." (Eph. 2:10, KJ) When we take allegiance to this pledge we bear the badge of Christ's helper; big or small our contributions spread and advance God's work. "Lay up yourselves treasures in heaven...." (Matt. 6:20, KJ) Through our good deeds we help other people lay up treasures in heaven. Then they can count "The Waves of Blessings" and "The Whispering Hope of God." "Be ye transformed by the renewing of what is good and acceptable and perfect Will of God." (Rom. 11:2, KJ) Our efforts and good works are to be inclusive to that precept.

God's commandments tell us to love others as we love ourselves. Why would a devote Christian want to hide or hoard their God ordained gift to humankind. It certainly would be contrary to God's expectations. Furthermore, there is the Great Commission found in (Matt.28:19-20, KJ) "Go ye therefore and teach all nations (peoples), baptizing them in the name of the Father and of the Son, and the Holy Ghost: teaching them to observe all things whatsoever I have commanded you ...." By God's commandment through our good works we are baptizing our fellow friends with the gift that God baptized us with. Therefore, I draw the conclusion that because of this instruction, Jesus expects us to utilize the gift that is inborn to infuse it into our works. Our personal works are inherent to that assignment. "This is a faithful saying, and these things I will that thou affirm constantly that they which have believed in God might be careful to maintain "Good Works" These things are good and profitable unto men." (Titus 3:8, KJ) "And let us also learn to maintain good works for necessary uses, that they be not unfruitful: (Titus 3:14, KJ) "....and I will shew thee my faith by my works." (James 2:18, KJ) "Ye see them how by works man is justified, and not by faith only." (James 2:24, KJ) "For as the body without the spirit is dead, so faith without works is dead also." (James 2:26, KJ) If we in fact live by faith in the spirit and image of Christ then we become a messenger in His name. Now the question can be asked "Is there a reward for having obeyed the Great Commission through our good works? The book of Revelations tells us that there is a spiritual compensation for our deeds while dwelling on earth."....and they were judged, every man according to their "works." (Rev. 20:13,KJ) "....and I will give unto everyone of you according to your "works." (Rev. 2:23,KJ)

Jesus said "Unless you see signs and wonders you will in no way believe." (John 4:48, KJ) Hopefully, this has been reflected and demonstrated by my writings and my hands. Often when we are concentrating on our works it affords us the opportunity to grasp the meaning and depth of God's creative genius and grace in us. We begin to more readily internalize the blessings of our gifts. Through our works we witness the invisible at work. "Therefore, we do not lose heart, even though our outward man is perishing, yet the inward man is being renewed day by day." (2 Cor. 4:16, KJ) As we show forth our faith it is unveiled in our gifted works. Although what we see is temporary, it does help prepare our hearts, minds, and soul for the future journey ahead. For there is a correlation between faith and works. God wants us to learn from each other. For we are his workmanship.

Infolded into this essay are the fruits of labor in designing and fabrication of stained glass religious pieces of work pertaining to Christiandom. They are an integral part of the theme of this book "The Wonder of it All." It takes thirty to forty hours of time to complete each picturesque theme. The theme of each piece encapsulates a message and visual way to artistically communicate with other people. Because it requires a significant amount of indulgence to finish such projects, it therefore gives the mind the freedom to dwell on our Heavenly Father, our Heavenly Host, our Creator, our Redeemer, as well as eternal hope. Christ's voluntary act on the sacrificial tree takes on a new perspective. It initiates and inspires the desire to delve into that theme in our lives. That being "The Wonder of it All." "You shall find the Lord, your God, if you seek with all heart and soul." (Deu. 4:29, KJ) Through our works we can come closer to establishing a one on one or heart to heart connection with our Lord. Out of works there is a resultant. In addition, it many times provided the atmosphere to escape from the unpleasantness associated with the unfortunate realities of life. Though the spirit of Christ is invisible, it does appear visible in our works for other people to see. Essentially, it becomes a testimony of our faith to encourage the non-beleiver or the neophyte Christian. It represents our thread being woven into the fabric of God's Kingdom. It becomes food for thought. What is the justification for doing so, as it applies to our good deeds? Jesus said "Don't stop him, because anyone who uses my name to do powerful things will not easily say evil things about me." (Mark 9:39,KJ) "But also look at the faith, in whose name is the work done?" (Matt. 7:17, KJ) Jesus was accepting of this man's work because it was done in the name of Christ. His grace says that is enough. It comes down to our integrity with Christ. "For everone who asks receives, and he who seeks finds, and to him who knocks it will be opened." (Matt. 7:7,KJ) To some degree God has opened the window so that I can observe "The Wonder of it All." "O Lord, thou art my my God; I will exalt thee, I will praise they name, for thou hast done wonderful things." (Isiah 25:1, KJ) "The generous soul will be made rich, and he who waters will also be watered himself." (Proverbs 11:25, KJ) "For he that in these things serveth Christ is acceptable to God, and approved of men. Let us therefore follow after the things which make for peace, and things wherewith one may edify another." (Rom. 14:18,19, KJ)"Let everyone of us please his neighbor for his good to edification." (Rom. 15:2, KJ) "Now the God of patience and consolation grant you to be like minded toward the other according to Jesus Christ. (Rom.15:5, KJ) "Now the God of hope fill you with joy and peace in believing that ye may abound in hope, through the power of the Holy Ghost." (Rom.15:13,KJ).

Perhaps it would be of interest to take each stained glass of work and interpret each theme. There is an old saying "A picture is worth a thousand words." So is the case with picturesque colorful renditions in stained glass to hang in windows as reminders of God's grace to us. What follows is a description of how each stained glass image relates to Christianity.

1.   GOD IN THE MIDST OF CREATION - WITH US EACH DAWNING: This simulates the fact that through God's creative genius he created all things. The Bible is there to remind us that it is our source for learning about His magnificence. Also, that God's Word is integral to life on earth. It also depicts the Holiness of His Spirit that dwells with us each hour of every day. His presence gives assurance of His faithfulness. He gave us a temporary earthly dwelling place for survial as well as our playground. Such gracious blessings are beyond words or expression. We are to be mindful of this and praise Him with our gratitude.

2.   GOD'S LOVE STORY: The Bible truly is God's message of love to each of us. His words were written to not only tell us that, but also to convey to us His expectations while we live on earth. Through His precepts and principles of living He encourages us to regain our spiritual relationship with Him

through His Son, Jesus Christ. He through His Son's redemptive power provides the opportunity to dwell with Him for eternity by faith. Where we entrust our future to him.

3.   THE LADDER OF FAITH: Faith is developed by reading the Bible. Piece by piece God develops in us a belief in Christianity. Faith is not instaneous, it is built over a period of time. It is an ever on going and growing process. Like the building blocks of knowledge in education, faith is built on a foundation of beliefs. That foundation is learning how to infuse the principles of "In God We Trust" as we progress through life. It is like climbing a ladder one rung at a time. No, we can't climb a ladder to dwell in heaven. However, we can elevate our beliefs in Jesus Christ to the point that when he fulfills his promises, he will descend from the clouds and say "Welcome To My Fathers Domain!".

4.   THE WONDER OF IT ALL: It truly is a wondrous thing about the Son of God willfully and voluntarily giving us spiritual hope through his act on the cross. The white robe hangs on the cross as a reminder of the genuiness and purity of his promise. It is beyond measure and comprehension the degree to which his sacrifice for our transgressions. The white cloak drapped over the cross symbolizes that Christ doesn't dwell on earth with humankind anymore. He was risen and resurrected to sit on the throne with his Father in heaven. Jesus uttered the words that we too can be with him in heaven when we through death discontinue our life on earth. By him, through him, and his salvation we can expect a guarantee of eternal life. The depth of that love is unquestionable.

5.   I AM YOUR SALVATION: God's Word reminds us that if we expect eternal life it is only by his grace that we gain entrance to a heavenly realm everlasting. We must be granted forgivenss through his salvation of our souls. It becomes an entitlement through the redemptive powers and grace of our creator. Thus, he takes on the title "Savior." For we are saved by the grace of God. What an honor and privilege it is to be granted such certification in the Kingdom of God. It certainly is a wondrous

blessing. Now you know why I selected "The Wonder of it All" as the title of this book.

6. IN REMEMBRACE OF ME: When we have been granted the gift of salvation it behooves us to say "Thank You!" Communion in the church (body of Christ) provides us that opportunity. By partaking of the bread and wine we are reminded of his sacrifice for us. It is a public display of our gratitude for some thing we can't accomplish for ourselves. For we can't save ourselves. The jurisdiction for that power is in the hands of Jesus Christ, our Lord. Otherwise, it becomes an assumption and is worthless. He is our advocate and mediator to God the Father. He is the keeper of the gate to what God has promised us.

7. UNITY IN WORSHIP AND PRAYER: In Christ we become a family destined to do good works. In unison as brothers/sisters we march together for the benefit of each other. Through the commandments and scriptural passages He reminds us to worship and pray together for the common good of all. In doing so, we fortify each other and become recipients of those benefits. Our walk must be genuine for the sake of all. Otherwise, God will rebuke us. To live steadfast in our faith is a challenge. Living in harmony and concert helps each of us to carry our burdens. For each of us are care givers in the name of the Lord.

I fully understand that Christ bears the stamp of approval on these works. May he understand and accept the incentive for having done it. Needless to say "Some day he will tell me." Our good works are an important part of "The Wonder of it all."

UNITY IN WORSHIP AND PRAYER

CHAPTER 15:

THE END - CLOSING THOUGHTS

1 John 3:18 "My children, we should love people not only with words and talk, but by our actions and true caring".

In fact there will never be a closure in life. For Jesus Christ promises life ever lasting. While on earth there never will be an end to misfortune and suffering. It has been ingrained into humanity. It is by God's Will and grace that we will be transported through the good and bad times. Within us must dwell reliance on the creator for all things, there isn't any escape. For without God's magnificent Holy power we would not exist. Nor would we be granted the assignment and privilege to be His working advocate. For that is our purpose and responsibility as Christians.

It must be thoroughly realized and understood that this thesis of thoughts has not been consecrated by God or the Church other than the fact that all of us have the inalienable right, liberty and power of our faith to praise our Lord. The text of this writing is interwoven with scripture, words of authors, personal writings, pictures and, hopefully, the Spirit of Christ. The primary intent was to develop a composite of works that might be especially beneficial to non-believers as well as people who cope with a psychological disease called depression or disorientation to the expectations of God and/or life responsibilities. All of which creates a sense of being overwhelmed. Encompassed therein are a variety of reasons. I know, because I have been through it. Many times it is the lack of preparation for the demands of life coupled with lack of a foundation to cope effectively in the spiritual realm. This story, "The Wonder of it all" is to a large degree in reference to the struggle to become more stable, both spiritually as well as emotionally. Searching for God is a profound undertaking. Disappointments at every turn, hoping to see or hear His voice. God where are you ? I was wrestling with the invisible one. As I approached and worked through this experience a confused, frustrated and perplexed man ventured into unknown waters. When and where would things make sense in terms of goals in life to give me direction ? When would I find relief? Oh, I was very active which produced a condition where I was constantly preoccupied with responsibilities. The mind could not relax and focus on our creator and the spirituality to deal with Him. The answer constantly alluded me by encountering more challenges. God did not make sense for countless reasons. To numerous to mention.

Eventually, I began to explore God's creation, trying to gain insight to the wonders God has provided us. God created it all, so why not ? Perhaps by exploring it, it would reveal His presence. As an outdoors person I had plenty of evidence to work with. There was the beauty of a country meadow loaded with colorful flowers, a brook and wildlife. So, I put pen to paper and started writing poems. All of which appear in this book. All the themes were inspired by God's gifts to us. The more I wrote, the more I marveled at God's Creative Genius and magical power. Yet, always giving Him the credit. There in, hopefully, to discover His ways and the spirit by which He relates to us. As I probed further, I began to expand those themes in accordance to scripture. They became analogies to make an interpretation or connection to God's presence in our life. Thus revealing the true nature of God, the spirit of omnipotence, omniscience and omnipresence. Of course, we discover that in the Word of God as we learn. However, some people require more of a visual clue to grasp what is being explained. Teaching methodologies or techniques are many times critical to comprehension. Over time God's image began to take shape. There formed a realization and sense that He not only touches us outwardly but that His spirit can be manifested in us, through Jesus Christ. The parables of Jesus Christ are good examples. Basically, by adopting His spirit and modify our ways to coincide with his ways, we live in Christ.

Now as for the content of this book "The Wonder of it all". In life the sharing of ideas and experiences provide us with information to build the furture on as we walk together. This is particularly true in the scientific or medical profession. We learn from each other. So it is that impetus that encouraged me to write this story. It relates to personal as well as spiritual struggles. Depression can be a formedable foe. We can't turn off the switch and make it go away. It must be methodologically chiseled away to expose the nature of the person in which it harbors. What transpired and emerged from that encounter with the invisible one is the resultant of my quest to find God. The Father, The Son and The Holy Spirit. Though invisible, He has a profound influence on our lives.

Some religious practices hold us in bondage by imposing strict and rigid requirements. We are not fenced in ! An old song would be appropriate here, "Don't fence me in". We inherit the liberty to accept Christ Jesus into our hearts. Like the wind we breath it in and breath it out. That is the profound beauty of Christianity. Christ does not limit the degree to which our spirit can soar or the degree that it stirs our conscience. If that were true, then a hymn, poem or a Christian testimony would have never been expressed. It is through these things that reveals the Christian spirit at work. Christ anionts us with the spirit. We become a vehicle to spread the good news. There is the traditional method (orthodoxy). Yes, we must accept God's Words, for he dictates the standards to stir our conscience. What we internalize gives us the spirit for our doings and our goings. It instills the inspiration to sing, to praise and write. Through "The Wonder of it all" we are released to fly free as an eagle and free to praise our creator. Capture and cage it, the spirit will never be allowed to grow. It will not reach its maturity or its destiny. Giving thanks to where ever it soars.

"Blessed are the people who know the joyful sound! They walk, O Lord, in the light of your countenance. In your name they rejoice all day long, and in Your righteousness they are exalted. For you are the glory of their strength." (Psalm 89:15,16 IBML)

"As every man hath received the gift, even so minister the same one to another, as good stewards of the manifold grace of God." (1 Peter 4:40,KJ)

"....for it is God who works in you both to will and to do for His good pleasure." (Phil. 2:13, KJ)

From where does the inspiration to write come from (the source) ? An invisible force that we all possess. Who among the prophets taught us how to write prayers and/or poems to God ? David, the psalmist. God's messenger to humanity of how to relate to God in the narrative format as well as poetic verse. God expects us to express our thoughts to Him. Thus, revealing our petitions for our spiritual growth as well as God's given gifts to serve Him. A Christian life is truly "The Wonder of it all". Hymn: Open my eyes, that I may see". The bottom line is to let our Christian faith be an example unto others. In other words, as the hymn implies "Let it shine." All God wants us to do is acknowledge Him and tell others of its merits. "For with the heart one believes unto righteousness, and with the mouth confession is made to salvation. For the scripture says "Whoever believes in him will not be put to shame." (Rom. 10:10,13 KJ)

Let us look at what Jesus said in Mark 9:39 "Don't stop him, because anyone who uses my name to do powerful things will not easily say evil things about me. "For whosoever shall give a cup of water to drink in my name because ye belong to Christ, verily I say unto you, he shall not lose his reward." (Mark 9:41, KJ) Production is more important than pedigree. The fruit is more important than the name of the orchard. If the person is bearing fruit, be grateful. Max Lucado. "A good tree can not produce bad fruit, (see Mat. 7:17). But also look at the faith. In whose name is the work done " ? Jesus was accepting of this man's work because it was done in the name of Christ. His grace says that is enough. It comes down to our integrity with Christ.

Perhaps the inclusion of two poems written will help further support and justify my way (style) to draw attention to Christ Jesus. The poem titled "Come and See" is an invitation to know and understand God. The poem "Awaken The Soul" is to bring into awareness and focus that we all have a soul and God owns it. Jesus Christ awakened humankind to the revelation of forgiveness and eternal life. Awareness stirs the conscience to hopefully open the door to invite a person to

"Come and See" and let Jesus knock on the door. So that they, too, can sing the hymns "How Great Thou Art" and "Amazing Grace." "But without faith it is impossible to please Him." (Heb. 11:6,KJ) Every poem that indwells is a blessing in comparison to the yesteryears. Let us rejoice in that blessing. Christianity is more than obedience, it gives us the imspiration and freedom to sing, to worship, to volunteer, to inspire others or to write to fulfill the needs of an individual. Like Paul, these are moments in the dessert to escape and learn how to let a sense of His presence stir our conscience, which then allows thoughts to formulate. To grasp hold of the moment and reveal the feelings that transpire.

As Christians we are on assignment to "draw attention" to God. Draw attention to Jesus Christ. Draw attention to the workings of the Holy Spirit. Draw attention to a new way of life. Draw attention to the redemptive powers of our Savior. Draw attention to the promise of everlasting life. Draw attention to the gospel so that Pastors can teach them the gospel truth. There in lies the purpose of praise, hymns and writings (poems). The purpose is to draw attention to the glory of God. That is the "clincher".

"That they should seek the Lord if happily they might feel after him, and find him, though he be not far from every one of us.")Acts 17:27, KJ) Psalm 139:23 "Search me, O God, and know my heart!." (Psalm 139:23, IBML)Through our works we examine and search our worthiness in the eyes of God. Engaging in such endeavors bears spiritual fruit. Will our performance display an honest, heartfelt and genuine desire to mold our motives through God and our given abilities ? When the chronicles of our efforts and achievements are reviewed and measured by our fellow man, will they be praise worthy and trustworthy ? Were the accomplishments for the benefit of all. Was it for selfish gain or was it exploitation of God for profitability ? In God's realm of thinking our gifts are to be shared for the physical and spiritual well beings of all people. Perhaps the "Golden Rule" applies here, "Do unto others as you would have them do unto you". Are the works done to show forth the inherent aspects of God in our lives as well as our faith ? Does it draw attention to our Lord and give Him the credit ? This is fundamental to the enrichment of our purpose for living. "Having gifts that differ according to the grace given to us, let us use them." ((Rom. 12:6, KJ)God knows our needs. Searching the realm of "The Wonder of it all" we can fill the empty holes in our spiritual life. We soon learn the He will provide. Also, we learn that the Christian faith is an on going process. We can never match God's wisdom. Each day offers something new in the annals of God's Kingdom. We come to realize that it is a life long adventure. As with all expeditions new discoveries refresh our minds and strengthens our spiritual faith to continue on to the reward. Each of us writes a personal journal of our relationship with the Holy anointed one. ".....asking God to fill us with the knowledge of His Will through all spiritual wisdom and understanding." (Col. 1:9, KJ) How can we discern the answers and fulfillment of that statement if it is not by the gifts we have inherited and offer it in the name of our Lord ? He openly accepts what we can give within the limitations of our capabilities. Hebrews 4:12 "For the Lord is living and active.... and is a discerner of the thoughts and intentions of our hearts." (Heb. 4:12,KJ) "So we speak, not to please men, but to please God who tests our hearts." (1 Thess. 2:2, IBML) So we speak, not to please men, but to serve human kind while the spirit of the Lord leads us. As we walk step by step along the path of "The Wonder of it all" we begin to grasp more thoroughly how we can serve our fellow brothers and sisters. We recognize that we are part of a brotherhood. Each striving to perfect him/herself for the benefit of all. Romans 8:5 "The Spirit itself beareth witness with our spirit, that we are the children of God." (Rom. 8:16, KJ) The will to explore God's treasures is the spirit at work. I can remember a saying directed toward me when I was active in church affairs. He/she would say "The spirit of the Lord is working in you". I have come to grips with the grace of our Lord by writing this book. As inadequate as it may be to serve justice to our creator, master and redeemer. "I can do all things in him who strengthens me." (Phil. 4:13, KJ) Each new insight to God's character and bountiful provisions gradually formed the mosiac pattern of thoughts in these writings. "Be steadfast, immovable, always abounding in the work of the Lord, knowing that in the Lord your labor is not in vain." (1 Cor. 15:58, KJ) "That ye might walk worthy of the Lord unto all pleasing, being fruitful in every good work, and increasing in the knowledge of God." (Col. 1:10, KJ)

ADMISSION

I do not profess myself as being filled with the Holy spirit. Nor do I claim to be a Bible scholar, other than what God has bestowed on me and represented in my works. I am just the average citizen of our country in God's creation seeking to know God better and attempt to please His expectations of me. I do so to magnify His name. I'm only a speck in humanity and a moment in time. But the Lord granted us the honor and privileged to speak His name. And through our Christian deeds to glorify "The Wonder of it all". The writing of this has been a spiritual encounter to prepare my heart, mind and soul for Jesus Christ.

There still exists unanswered questions that will probably go unsolved because of the nature of man verses the mysterious nature of God. There are questions which I don't think He wants us to know. I think that he realizes that if we knew all the answers to creation, life and God's diety, it would take away the mystery and the wonderment in life. Faith would be dissolved into a lack of desire for futuristic thinking. It would remove from us the challenge of discovery. Life is analogous to competition in sports, such as running a race. If we knew before hand whom the winner is going to be, the challenge wouldn't be filled with fun, anticipation, wonder and glory. It would destroy our desire to dream, to hope, to pursue and achieve goals in life. All of which are fundamental to the endowment of faith, which ultimately becomes the underpinning basic principle of the indwelling spirit. And, which in turn shows forth the tenets of Christianity. We would be void of the essential ingredient in our life to yearn for and reach for tomorrow. God wants us to strive for, work for and earn the rights to eternal life. Our faith and our deeds will be judged. He wants us to be surprised, to rejoice and to be filled with joy when we become recipients of the rewards of Christianity. A Christmas gift or birthday present wouldn't be much of a surprise if we knew before hand. Christ's gift of eternal life on heavens shore is to be sought with anticipation, great expectation and most importantly, with a deep sense of honesty, sincerity and reverence. An honored surprise bestowed upon us with

His own personal blessing. He wants the pleasure of granting us the certidficate which states; "Welcome to Heaven!"

".....that our God would count you worthy of this calling, and fuffill all the good pleasures of His goodness, and the work of faith with power."   (Thess.1:1 1, JH) As we nuture our faith our heart beat grows stronger in the Lord. I can't warble like a song bird, but my hands can sing just as loud. There is a reciporcal to God's love, it is our expression through our works. It is measured out according to our knowledge of God. To please God is the common denominator to this endeavor. God ignited the spiritual fuel. The scriptures tell us that there is a season for everything. Hopefully, this book is my season to reveal my reasons for honoring the creator of my life and the faith he has instilled. Faith without works is a dead-end street. "Walk worthy of the vocation where with you are called." (Eph. 4:1, KJ) Our works are like a garden, seeds planted to give nourishment to other people.

This resumé of thoughts has been entrusted into the hands of our Lord. May it be blessed and bear fruit. May the works glorify and magnify the name of our Lord. My intent is to walk in partnership with Christ to share and spread the good news. As Jesus said to his followers "You shall be my witnesses." It is expected to take notice of the name of the Son of God. We all are on a mission with God given gifts for the sake of other people. All of humanity has experienced "A Searching Passage" seeking God's grace." Rejoice in "The Wonder of it All." During your passage sit down and write to your Lord. You'll not only discover yourself, but the greatness of the Holy One who calls us His children.

PASS IT ON

It is my sincere hope that you enjoyed reading this collection of thoughts. The challenge of writing it has been a rewarding experience. This book is an indication that because of God's variety of blessings they afford the opportunity to discover innovative ways to acknowledge and credit the Most High Priest. It has not been my intention to exploit God's Word or the works of other people. All has been written to inspire people to study "The Wonder Of It All". May it shed light on the invisibility of our creator. May it, furthermore, instill a deeper sense of gratitude for "God's creative genius and Christ's redemptive grace". For without God we would not exist and the Spirit of Jesus would not indwell our hearts. Praise the workings of the Holy Spirit. May you be free as the eagle to acknowledge God's blessings in our lives. It is free, however, it should not be taken for granted. Climb the "Ladder of Faith" and enjoy the "Waves of Blessings" as well as listen to "God's Whispering Hope." Hopefully, I have caught a glimpse of God. It will surprise you what you'll find. May the mediations of my heart and mind be acceptable in the sight of God and blend with yours as well. Philippians 4:8 "Finally, brethren, whatever things are true, whatever things are noble, whatever things are just, whatever things are pure, whatever things are lovely, whatever things are of good report, if there is any virtue and if there is anything praiseworthy - mediate on these things." (Phil. 4:8,KJ) 1 Thessalonians 1:3 "Remembering without ceasing your work of faith, and labor of love, and patience of hope in our Lord, Jesus Christ, in the sight of God, our Father." (Thess. 1:3,KJ) Hopefully I have articulated inspirational thoughts fundamental to the spirit of Christianity. At least that is God's given assignment. That is to share our cup of faith. The End.

TAKEN FOR GRANTED

Taking for granted the days of our lives,
one day at a time God gives.
Seldom thoughts about from where we came,
God thinks, "What a sinful shame."

Onward we march seeking personal goals,
as life rapidly unfolds.
Day to day writing our life's story,
controlling forces which our soul destroy.

From childhood to adulthood,
demands we withstood,
Education or skills to learn,
working for money to earn.

Families to raise and bills to pay,
responsibilities every day.
Other interests attract our attention,
so many there are to mention.

Living in a world of varied issues,
Oh, the confusion that ensues.
Social and political problems world wide,
all impedes our stride.

Forces which become all consuming,
there tasks we are assuming.
The spirit of our soul becomes lost,
what a dreadful cost.

Perhaps God looks down in confusion,
knowing our need for His intercession.
Taking for granted the days of our lives,
one day at a time God gives.

Each dawning should have His guidance,
each glowing with radiance.
Each day we take for granted,
none can be recanted.
Cherish those He has granted,
respond by not taking God for granted.

RG

LEAN ON YOUR UNDERSTANDING

That God was the creator of all things.

That God gave birth to the human race.

That there is only one God.

That God is a sovereign God.

That God is the almighty.

That God is the Holy One and Most High.

That God controls all things.

That God is omniscient.

That God is omnipotent.

That God is omnipresent.

That God is a just God.

That God gave us the Ten Commandments.

That God is righteous.

That God's Word is the truth.

That God is a loving God.

That God gave His only begotten Son, Jesus Christ.

That humankind are sinful people.

That God is angered at deceit, greed, selfishness, murder. Etc.

That Christ Jesus lived to teach us how to live righteously.

That Christ Jesus voluntary act of crucifixion on the cross gave us salvation for the remission of sin.

That Christ Jesus had victory over death and passes it on to us

That we must confess our sins to Christ Jesus.

That we must confess and ask for Jesus forgiveness.

That we too must demonstrate forgiveness. See the Lord's Prayer and poem titled "Forgiveness".

That Jesus Christ loved us enough to free us from the bondage of sin.

That Jesus Christ promised us life eternal if we believe and follow him.

That Jesus Christ attaches a condition to his everlasting love, that is to be reborn and baptized in His name.

That Jesus Christ has the authority of redemptive powers.

That it is only through Jesus Christ that we can expect to see His Father.

That God gave us freedom of choice as to whether or not we continue in our life separated from Him.

That it is by Jesus Christ mercy and grace that we are saved.

That God told us that there is a hell for the unsaved.

That God created heaven.

That God knows our every thought and deed.

That God told us that it is through "FAITH" that we receive the grace of God.

That we are to worship God and praise Him for our blessings.

That Christ Jesus will hear all our supplications (prayers) and to pray unceasing.

That we are to pray to God with adoration.

That life is an impossible verture (mission) without Jesus Christ.

That God expects us to take on the likeness (image) of Jesus Christ.

That we are to love our neighbors as ourselves.

That we are to spread the gospel and fruits of the Holy Spirit world wide.

That we are to receive salvation, baptism and Holy Communion.

That going to church, being good, reading the Bible or make generous offerings does not give us salvation, it is Christ's redemptive grace. It is free.

God wrote letters to us. Write letters to Him acknowledging His faithfulness and don't conceal your faith. It is essential for our eternal survival.

That life on earth is not a dead end street.

That our purpose in life is to serve God.

That God is "How Great Thou Are".

That God proclaims all of the above.

REJOICING

When God created the universe, He rejoiced.

When God created life on earth, He rejoiced.

He was pleased when He looked at the animals,
fish, birds, plants, He rejoiced.

When He created man and woman, He rejoiced.

Then they betrayed His loving gift, saddened was His
rejoicing.

Then God made a way to reclaim His children.
For each soul he reclaims, He rejoices.

Then He gave humankind a choice,
Reject Me or follow Me, then I'll rejoice.

In salvation there is rejoicing,
for it units us with God, rejoice.

He promises everlasting life,
Our hearts should over flow with rejoicing.

Always remember that it pleases God and
restores His rejoicing.

Rejoice, rejoice, rejoice, for it is God's Will.
Our hope in heaven, He will fulfill.

For rejoicing is found in the book of life,
It is found in "The Wonder of it all".

RG

Paul said "Rejoice in the Lord always, Again, I say, rejoice !" (Phil. 4:4, JH)

Psalm 100: "Make a joyful shout to the Lord, all the lands !" (Psalm 4:4,KJ) Serve the Lord with gladness; Come before His presence with singing. Know that the Lord, He is God; It is He who made s and not we ourselves.

We are His people and the sheep of His pasture.
Enter into His gates with thanksgiving,
And into His courts with praise,
Be thankful to Him and bless His name.
For the Lord is good;
His mercy is everlasting,
And His truth endures to all generations".

" Make a joyful shout to God, all the earth!" (Psalm 66:1,KJ)
Sing out the honor of His name;
Make His praise glorious.
Say to God "How awesome are Your works !".

Note: The title and context of this book surrounds that acclaim.

"And my soul shall be joyful in the Lord." (Psalm 35:9,KJ)

"Oh come, let us sing to the Lord!" (Psalm 95:2,KJ)
Let us come before His presence with thanksgiving.
Let us shout joyfully to Him in psalms".

In Christ we all have our individual psalm to sing, whether it be writing hymns, poems, stories to be told as a means to witness or design things to bring recognition to our Lord. Hopefully, this collection of thoughts will promote rejoicing. Like the eagle, let the spirit reign free so we all can enjoy it.

SHALL WE REMINISCE?

Of Christ shall we reminisce,
His spirit, an ageless renascence.

When Christ came into this world, there was rejoicing.
When Christ lived, there was rejoicing.
When Christ died, there was rejoicing.
Count this blessing with great rejoicing.

Christ our savior, prince of peace,
to him, your soul release.

"Only one life, twill soon be past;
Only what's done for Christ will last" C.T.Scott

Lift up your eyes unto the hills,
from whence you'll find His will.

To this dream steadfast hold and cherish,
those without, their vision shall perish.

Christ guides us along the pathway,
Today, tomorrow and always.

Take time to reminisce,
Like the spring time, vibrant colors luminance.

Your soul refresh, as you reminisce.

RG

WHAT A FRIEND WE HAVE IN JESUS

What a Friend we have in Jesus,
all our sins and griefs to bear!
What a privilege to carry,
everything to God in prayer!
O what peace we often forfeit,
O what needless pain we bear.
All because we do not carry,
everything to God in prayer!

Have we trials and temptations?
Is there trouble any where?
We should never be discouraged;
take it to the Lord prayer.
Can we find a friend so faithful,
who will all our sorrows share?
Jesus knows our every weakness;
take it to the Lord in prayer.

Are we weak and heavy laden?
cumbered with a load of care?
Precious Savior, still our refuge;
Take it to the Lord in prayer.
Do thy friends despise, forsake thee?
Take it to the Lord in prayer.
In His arms He'll take and shield thee;
Thou wilt find a solace there.

The Celebration Hymnal

WAVES OF BLESSINGS

I sat on the seashore today,
looking at the horizon far away.
Where the blue sky meets the sea,
God's blessing of vision, so thankful to see.

Wondering where the waves come from,
all topped with white foam.
Their shapes cast against aqua green,
instilling a sense to relax and enjoy the scene.

Waves appear in abundant number,
one replaces the other in repetitious thunder.
I sat and watched as I slumber,
then these thoughts I remember.

God's blessings come from beyond the horizon,
waves of blessings as life goes on.
Gracious gifts now to ponder.
To His grace we grow fonder.

The waves of life inherent to His creation,
for this we submit our adoration.
The waves of family and friends,
through us His spirit transcends.

A multitude of other waves in review,
as more waves come into view.
The wave of love as Christ makes His adoptions,
endless as the waves flow with constant motion.

Listen, hear and see the waves,
even though life's woes enslave.
Look to the horizon to see more,
as the waves roll to our shore.
So set on the beach reminiscing,
and count the waves of blessings.

Though the waves appear in restless artistry,
they instill a sense of pleasantry.
The curiosity to look beyond whence they came,
to God's mysterious majesty.

To give Him the fame,
and through His grace liberty.
When waves of blessings wash up on our shore,
give thanks more and more.

RG

BLESSINGS COME OUR WAY

I awake each morning, God's blessings to view,
they come as a generous flow.
To my senses they ensue,
in our hearts it is quite a show.

You designed an earth enshrined,
Your glorious display is our clue.
For you have been generous and kind,
We learn this when setting in pew.
Your grace does feed our soul,
it feeds our spirit and make it new.

Even the animals, birds and flowers,
extend a "Thank you" your way.
For you are with us each day,
without you these blessings would not stay.

You bathe us with your spirit,
washing away our sorrows.
Giving us strength, if we admit,
helping us to face all the tomorrows.

In these things we delight,
for they bring us pleasures.
Truly a magnificent sight,
we applaud your treasures.

Blessings that come our way,
each and every day.

RG

"....for your heavenly Father knoweth that
we have need of all these things." (Matt.6:32)

Beautiful Saviour!

Beautiful are
HIS WAYS,
HIS WORKS,
HIS WORDS,
and
HIS WONDERS.

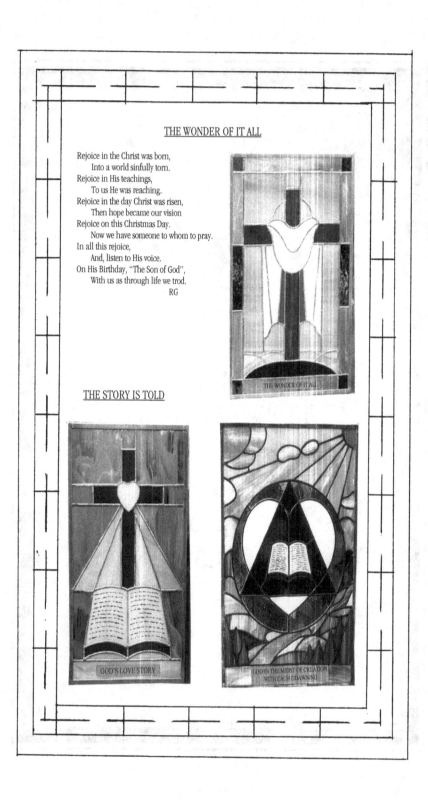

THE WONDER OF IT ALL

Rejoice in the Christ was born,
    Into a world sinfully torn.
Rejoice in His teachings,
    To us He was reaching.
Rejoice in the day Christ was risen,
    Then hope became our vision
Rejoice on this Christmas Day.
    Now we have someone to whom to pray.
In all this rejoice,
    And, listen to His voice.
On His Birthday, "The Son of God",
    With us as through life we trod.
             RG

THE STORY IS TOLD

THE WONDER OF IT ALL

GOD'S LOVE STORY

GOD IN THE MIDST OF CREATION
WITH EACH DAWNING

THE CHRISTMAS TREE

Tonight I sat by the Christmas tree,
letting the mind run free.
The ornaments and lights brightly glow,
and memories start to flow.

Remembering Christmas's of distant past,
recollections in pleasantries cast.
Some are vivid, while others are foggy,
the years tend to blend and I get groggy.

Then I start counting the lights;
letting the lights represent a memory,
as the tree lights twinkle in the night.
The lights are not enough for the count,
the ornaments remind of "Memories"
Amazed at the amount!

I fondly recall family and friends,
their love and friendship, we have come to depend.
Friends are one of God's gifts,
our spirit they help us to lift.
These thoughts dwell in my heart,
in life you have become a special part.

Then I ponder and realize,
as I internalize.
Christ is the eternal light,
shinning day and night.
For He gives hope to our souls,
we, a person, a child of God on His scroll.
For Christ's birth touches our hearts,
a gift never to replace or depart.
Jesus, how can we neglect so great a gift ?

Atop the tree is a star,
reminding us of God's gift from afar.
Of this the ancients told,
so the rest of the world could behold.
For a Savior is born,
to rescue the world sinfully torn.
Christmas celebrates His birth,
and, His love to give us rebirth.
May the Christmas Season,
remind us of the special reason.

RG

"But without faith it is impossible to please Him." (Heb. 11"6,KJ)

THANKSGIVING

Oh precious Father, as we bow,
before Thy throne today,
We count the blessings,
thou hast showered upon our way.

The comfort of our humble homes,
our health and happiness.
The strength provided each day,
to meet the strain and stress.

We thank Thee for Thy precious Son,
who brought salvation free,
And for this mighty land of ours,
"A land of liberty!".

So Lord, help us to give Thee Thanks,
for all that we hold dear,
Not only on Thanksgiving Day,
but each day of the year.

RG

THE NEW YEAR

By God's grace we visit a new year,
into its events, He permits us to peer.

The sun will rise and fall,
just has He planned.
Allowing us to stand tall,
in faith as Christ waves His majestic wand.

In His time He'll measure out each day,
so that we can work and play.
We'll discover both bad and good,
history tells us that should be understood.

Moments of sadness and gloom,
others will produce a gleeful smile
As Christ walks with us each mile,
God's Word tells us this we can assume.

Now for those resolutions,
and the opportunity for absolution.
Renewed by Christ's forgiving grace.
giving us hope to move forward at a steady pace.

May the New Year abound with blessings to count.
Then be surprised at the amount.

RG

HYMN: ANOTHER YEAR IS DAWNING

Another year is dawning;
Dear Father, let it be,
In working and in waiting.
Another year with Thee;
Another year of progress,
Another year of proving,
Thy presence all the days.

Another year of mercies,
of faithfulness and grace;
Another year of gladness,
in the shinning of The face;
Another year of learning,
upon The loving breast.
Another year of trusting,
of quiet, happy rest.

Another year of service,
of witnessing The love;
Another of training,
for holier work above.
Another year is dawning;
Father, let it be,
On earth or else in heaven,
Another year for Thee.

The Celebration Hymnal

WHAT DO YOU SEE ?

With eyes closed;
Look into the future,
what do you see ?

Do you see material things ?
Do you see cars, motor cycles or houses?
or do you see darkness or just nothing ?

Yes, these thoughts we ponder,
and to Christ's promises we grow fonder.
In life, this theme we wonder,
to grasp and say "Thank You" to the founder.

RG

MAY IT HELP

I discovered things along the way,
hopefully, they'll help you on this day.

For life is worth while living,
let your faith provide the giving.
Don't let life get you down,
spirit up, please don't drown.

Though I am only human,
festering with flaws.
These thoughts within me remain,
and, there is purpose to my cause.

As God is my witness,
it may not be my best.
To some it may be nonsense,
although it helped me to face the test.

A story told in God's presence,
now ;you know the rest.
Hopefully you have been receptive,
For it gives a new perspective.

RG

Christ said, "It is finished".
"I will not cast you out"

"How shall we escape, if we neglect so great salvation?" (Heb. 2:3,KJ)
"Behold, I stand at the door and knock. If any man hears my voice, and
open the door, I will come into him." (Rev. 3:20,KJ)

A FRIEND

Special is a friend,
people on whom we depend.

The moments of sharing,
especially the caring.
Moments together passing the time away,
a blessing counted each day.

The gift of their love and kindness,
instilling a sense of gladness.
In times of need they are there,
helping our soul to bear.

They encourage in gentle voice,
and share in our rejoice.
They help us to smile,
making life worthwhile.

Friendship lasting over the years,
a bondage tried and dear.
Oh, how they warm the heart,
sad to see them depart.

The fond memories of friendship,
fill the sails of life's ship.
Thank God for a friend,
to walk with, to talk with, Friend to Friend.

RG

GOD'S WHISPERING HOPE

The Holy Spirit is Heaven's silent voice,
we hear it as our choice.
Listen to the whisper.

We become God's guest,
received at our request.
Listen to the whisper.

It touches our soul,
like winds' gentle flow.
Listen to the whisper.

In solitude we hear the message,
recorded in the Good Book passage.
Listen to the whisper.

The whisper is an encompassing force,
for assurance reach for the source.
Listen to the whisper.

Daily through life we trod,
living by the grace of God.
Listen to the whisper.

God's whispering hope,
gives the faith to cope.
Listen to the "Whisper".

RG

If we don's listen to God's whispering hope, then life is meaningless. And if we don't believe that our soul is homeward bound, then faith is worthless and futile. Our purpose for living becomes a tragedy. A dead end street, with Christ's promises being fruitless. It is our assignment and responsibility to draw attention" to God's Word, which fulfills not only His precepts and promises, but the interpretation of hymns sung and poems read, all of which reflects the workings of the indwelling spirit, hi other words " Christ's work" regardless of our inability to capture the full meanings and significance of "The Wonder of it All". Christ brought with Him "God's Whispering Hope" for all humankind. God's whispering hope was evident at Pentecost. It came in like the wind. That wind (spirit) has blown throughout humanity for over two thousand years. Christ's birth and death on the cross gave us salvation for the remission of sins. It is a covenant and promise. All is guaranteed in God's Word.

GOD IS NEAR

How do we know God is near,
as we daily go our way?
What possesses us to think He is there?
Or do we say he is here?

I see Him in all that surrounds,
I see Him in you and me.
Everywhere he abounds,
all we have to do is look and see.

In our hearts he is found,
to us he'll forever be.
To us he'll set the sails,
even when we are frail.

Yes, he is never far away,
united with every heart.
Trust in Him, day after day,
God is near and he" never depart.

To this dream take hold,
for your faith he will mold.

RG

"The Lord is close to everyone who prays to him.
To all who truly pray to Him." (Psalm 17:6)

A HEART OF LOVE

From where does love originate?
Given to us as a choice.
It is more than just fate,
it comes from God's voice.

It is to have and behold,
a gift of a special art.
It spreads as life unfolds,
helping to serve a special part.

It is essential for a Christian life,
it is God's will at work.
His grace through us uplifts,
where it goes it leaves a special mark.

What is the gift of love?
It is part of our Christian faith.
Given to others, free as a bird,
like the winds that blow.

Into the hearts of others,
we lift them with spirit low.
We are asked to plant special seeds,
that will grow into joyous deeds.

Lighting a glow in their hearts,
as our love we impart.
Serving our Lord and gracehood,
living in brother/sisterhood.

Making us dearer and nearer to our Lord,
love granted on his accord.
Surely this act we can afford,
as our cup of faith is poured.

This is our duty as Christian's,
to lend a helping hand.
for we live together on this land.

Forging ahead with God's heart of love.

RG

"And let us consider one another in order to stir up love and good.."
(Heb. 10:24)

HYMN: IT IS WELL WITH MY SOUL

When peace like a river attendeth my way,
when sorrows like sea bellows roll;
What ever my lot,
thou hast taught me to say,
It is well, it is well with my soul.

Though Satan should buffet,
though trials should come,
Let this blest assurance control;
that Christ hath regard for my help low estate,
And hath shed His own blood for my soul.

My sin, O, the bliss of this glorious thought,
my sin - not in assurance, not in part, but the whole,
is nailed to the cross,
And I bear it no more,
praise the Lord, praise the Lord, O my soul.

And, Lord, haste the day when,
the faith shall be sight,
The clouds be rolled back as a scroll,
the trumpet shall resound and the Lord shall descend.
Even so - it is well with my soul.

The Celebration Hymnal

OUR CHURCH

There you stand on the hill.
Steeple tall, how stately you are.
We who see, get a thrill.
Those who come, near and far.

In silence, alone you stand.
Things of the past you know,
In days of old, pastor manned.
Generations, you helped us grow.

If only you could tell us,
the stories of the past.
T'would be something to discuss,
with tales of blessed cast.

Your doors opened minds to the almighty.
Teachings of heavens view.
God's beacon, a lamp shinning brightly.
Promises learned while setting in pew.

You guide our spiritual soul,
so that all who see,
may reach their goal.
At journey's end, where we must be.

You guide us through calm and storm,
whatever the conflict might be.
Knowing we are safe and warm,
when we are there to see.

Our church, you bring romance to all.
We can't stray away from you.
We are ever at your beckoning call.
To you, we'll always be true.

You've stood there over 100 years.
And, we hope for hundreds more.
We relax and calm our fears,
when we enter your door.

So, thank you, for God's house,
and the blessings you bring.
Your gleaming sight, no man must douse.
For it makes our hearts to sing.

God bless our church!   RG

TIME FOR CHURCH

Sunday mom, Mom yells, "Time for church!"
In the car mom, dad, sisters and me, too.
Start the car, then off in a lurch,
Down the road, the neighbors, too.
The reason, God's message tried and true.

There's the church with congregation gathering,
time to worship and learn the gospels.
Steeple standing tall against the sky,
Christ's ascension is the reason why.

Stained glass windows pierce the walls,
glitter of color on pews fall.
Gothic windows depict Bible scenes,
pageant colors, yet serene.
If only this church could talk,
The history, the baptisms, the weddings, the wakes.

Usher's greeting with a friendly hand shake,
a program, now to a seat
The cross on the alter reminds, he died for our sake!
Flowers arranged ever so neat.

In the sanctuary there's something in the air,
God's spirit, ours to heir.
Organist on keyboard plays a tune of recognition,
in hymnal, voices sing in unison.

Pastor behind pulpit stands, heads bowed, he leads a prayer,
silence broken, a boy asks, Dad "Why is he praying?"
Humble words spoken in reverence,
transcending to seeks God's presence.

The offering, ushers now collect,
God's support, a prayer recollects.
From pulpit the pastor delivers a message,
glancing at Bible passages.

A story he interjects to make a point,
our soul, God's spirit to anoint.
Now the closure, the benediction,
God's guidance requested with conviction.

As we exit, the pastors hand we grasp,
A friendship, a hug, a loving clasp.
A gentile voice, a sparkle in his eye,
He says "Don't forget next Sunday, time for church!"

RG

OUR PASTOR

To you we come, our spirit low,
Troubles with our soul.
Your hand extended, a Christian gesture,
Gods servant is your measure.

With wisdom as your course,
Spiritual values as your source.
Our soul you gave direction,
Guided with your compassion.
Gods word became the foundation,

His spirit, the inspiration.
Our life given new meaning,
This you instill with your preaching.
Your friendship, truely I acknowledge,
Just as God's spirit reignth for eternity.

RG

P-A-S-T-O-R

The "P" stands for privilege.
A Privilege, God to represent.
His word, heaven sent.
Seeking who desire to repent,
A pledge, of fullest extent

The "A" stands for assignment.
Gods relevance, I must teach.
People of the world, many to reach.
Gods guidance daily I beseech,
This I do on Sunday preach.

The "S" stand for service.
To God's service, I am servant.
To his deed I gladly submit.
To his people I giveth comfort.
Peace, joy, glad tidings, I bring forth.

The "T" stands for trust.
In God's way you trust.
Congregation they too entrust.
Our guidance as you forward thrust.
Souls salvation, is our must.

The "O" stand for ordained.
An oath as Gods' minister.
Church doctrines you administer.
God's people, in assembly they worship,
As you portray Gods' friendship.

The "R" stands for reverence.
In pulpit you stand in reverence.
A message to those in attendance,
Praying with heartfelt earnest.
Our soul, God's spirit you hold firmest.
The cross, your vision of leadership.
Thank God for your pastorship.

RG

CHAPTER 16:

THE GIFT OF SCIENCE

By Roger Goodman

Some people have a misguided opinion about the relationship between science and religion. They think that science contradicts God's Will. As will be pointed out that is a big misconception. The Bible tells us that is a false interpretation. There is a significant connection between equations and God. Equations tell the story of God's earthly laws. One could say that God is the Great mathematical genius.

As Christians we know that God created the universe. God also designed the earth especially for humankind. The planet we call earth in reality is a space craft traveling through the solar system. As we go about our daily lives we are rotating in an orbit around the sun at a speed of 67,500 mph. Wow ! What a miraculous thing. God gave birth to the animals, birds and the flowers. And, yes, we human beings. The study of all things created by God is called the sciences. It is not a contradiction of God's plan, but an understanding of what God has given us.

Now some passages from the Bible to verify this point of view;

"Be fruitful and multiply and replenish the earth and subdue it." I shall restate the last two words, subdue it. That means subdue the Earth. That is what scientists have been doing for mankind for 1,500 years. (Gen. 1:18, KJ)

A question: "What do wise men do ?"

"The tongue of the wise useth knowledge aright." (Prov. 15:2, KJ)

"The lips of the wise disperse knowledge." (Prov. 15:7, KJ)

"Wisdom is before him that hath understanding." (Prov. 17:24, KJ)

"The words of man's mouth is as deep waters and the wellspring of wisdom as a flowing brook." (Prov. 18:4, KJ)

There is an old saying "A person can't learn unless he/she partakes of knowledge". Whether we are 16 years old or 76 years old, it is never to late to learn and understand God's creation. The Bible tells us that we are to understand God's works. God also instructs us to inform future generations. That means our children and our grandchildren. It is a life long assignment. In doing so, we satisfy the expectations of our maker.

God said "Neglect not the gift in thee". Scientists have the gift to understand God's Laws of Creation. We become the benefactors of their discoveries and inventions. The resultant is that we live a more comfortable and sophisticated life style than people did 1,500 years ago. All because of God's permissive will granted to us. Science is the study of God's creation. The science of God's natural laws. The sciences validate God's creative genius.

A.   The earth; "God's Gift To Us":
   1. Natural laws which few men understand. Most people take it for granted.
       Yet, we are the benefactors.
   2. This brief study fosters two things;
       a. A better understanding and further insight to God's Creation. Therefore, a deeper and more sensitive appreciation for what He has given us.
       b. Hymn: "Count Your Blessings One by One". Poem: "Waves of Blessings".
   3. Poem: "The Master's Hand".

a. Bible passage. "Praise to the sovereign Lord for His creation and His providence." (Psalm 104, KJ)

4. The omnipresence of God: God's spirit (will) is everywhere at the same time and is always in control.

5. Quote by Issac Newton: "We have explained the phenomena of the heavens. By the power of gravity, but have not assigned the cause of it all. This most beautiful system of the sun, planets and comets, could only proceed from the counsel and dominion of an intelligent and powerful being "Science had not ostracized God from the universe. Instead the creator always has been, was and would be every where thoughout His creation."

6. Eventual end of the world: Rudolf Clausius.

    a. The earth's energy system (entropy).

    b. Quote: "The universe must have started out being very tense and very organized; it was as though billions of years ago something or someone had built a superbly designed a spring-driven clock and had it wound it up good and tight. Like that clock, the universe was in the process of slowly winding down, slowly relaxing, slowly falling apart."

    c. Bible passage: Prophesy that all things will be made new. "Now I saw a new heaven and a new earth, for the first heaven and the first earth had passed away." (Rev. 21, KJ)

B. The invisible forces (unseen energy).

1. Light

    a. Natural light is invisible.

    b. We see colors as the result of light refraction or absorption that changes light wave frequencies.

2. Gravity: The force (God's glue) to hold the planets of the universe in relative position.

3. Centrifugal forces: Rotational energy.

4. Kinetic (stored) energy.

5. Heat energy.

6. Fluid (air, water, etc.) energy.

7. Electrical energy.

8. Magnetism.
9. Sound waves.
10. Atomic energy: Einstein's "Theory of Relativity." All matter has an atomic cohesiveness. Breaking the atomic bondage releases and creates tremendous energy. One lump of coal burning equals enough energy to light one light bulb for one hour. Mass energy conversion; atomic fission reaction equals enough energy to light one bulb for 1,680 billion hours.
11. Energy of life: Who can explain the forces of life. It certainly depicts God's creative genius when we look at the many forms of life. Our conclusion is that our God is a God of variety. His intelligence is beyond comprehension. Through the sciences we absorb a small portion of His greatness. The blessings He has bestowed on us is beyond measure. We trust in and are thankful for His benevolent Gifts. Therefore, we should honor, respect and praise His glory for His grace to us. Life, what a marvelous gift it is. Psalm 36.9 "For with you is the fountain of life."
12. God's omnipotent energy" Never seen ? Note: All energy sources are invisible, including the Holy Spirit of God (Jesus Christ).
    a. The indwelling invisible spirit. Our spirituality is shown forth in our faith, our actions and the things we do. The spirit causes us to incorporate God's gifts into our life.
    b. Bible passages: Jesus said "Abide in me I in you." (John 15:4,KJ "Hereby we know that he abideth in us by the spirit which he hath given us." (John 3:24)
    c. Question: Can we identify or quantify God's energy (power)?
    d. "The Lord is my light and my salvation." (Psalm 27:1, KJ) "For with you is the fountain of life." (Psalm 36:9, KJ)

GOD AND SPECULATION

"In the beginning God created the heavens, sun, moon, stars, etc., (placing emphasis on earth) and the spirit of God was hovering over the waters, (waters on the earth). Then God said let there be firmament. God's firmament formed the earth. (Gen. 1:1,2, KJ) "And the nations of those who are saved shall walk in the light, and the Kings of the "earth" bring glory and honor into it." (Rev. 21:24, KJ) Note the emphasis on earth. Between Genesis and Revelations the word "earth" is used 964 times. The word world is used 240 times. Now the definition of world. The world state; the earth with its inhabitants and all things on it, the concerns of the earth and its affairs. The word "universe" does not appear in the Strong's Exhaustive Concordance of the Bible. Therefore, the conclusion is drawn that God's Holy Word applies only to the earth and all things living on it. When Jesus was asked about salvation, he said "If it were not true, I would have told you so". If there is another planet that harbors life (people) then I firmly believe that He would have told us. To think otherwise is shear speculation. It takes things out of context of the truth that God has told us. It misrepresents what God has created. Therefore, it induces false information in the minds of neophyte Christians, and most importantly children. Do I believe that there are people living on another planet ? Absolutely not! Why ? Because I trust God enough to the point that "He would have told us.". Remember that He is the creator of all things. He is the one with all the answers, not us. I believe we must stay in the confines of what God has given us. For it is here on earth that we seek Christ's salvation, not in the cosmos. When we meet Jesus in heaven, will we see people from other planets ? No ! Praise God. There are two types of will in God's Kingdom. There is God's ordained will and God's permissive will. We were granted permissive will in the Garden of Eden. Speculation is playing games with God's righteousness. Yes, there is God's Will and He controls all things.

(119:10KJ) "With my whole heart I have sought You; Oh, let me not wander from your commandments (His Will). Your word I have hidden in my heart."

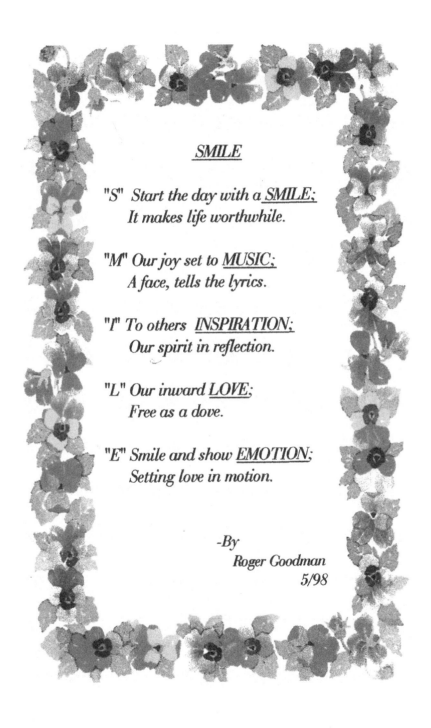

SMILE

"S" Start the day with a SMILE;
It makes life worthwhile.

"M" Our joy set to MUSIC;
A face, tells the lyrics.

"I" To others INSPIRATION;
Our spirit in reflection.

"L" Our inward LOVE;
Free as a dove.

"E" Smile and show EMOTION;
Setting love in motion.

-By
Roger Goodman
5/98

REFERENCES:

BOOKS AND AUTHORS

The Holy Bible: KJ

The Inspirational Study Bible by Max Lucado: IBML

The Celebration Hymnal by Integrity Music

The Purpose Driven Life by Rick Warren

In The Grip of Grace by Max Lucado

What's So Amazing About Grace by Phillip Yancy

When God Whispers Your Name by Max Lucado

Who I Am In Christ by Neil T. Anderson

The Jesus I Never Knew by Phillip Yancy

Peace With God by Billy Graham

A Mind For God by James Emery White

When God Doesn't Make Sense by James Dobson

The Road Less Traveled by M. Scott Peck, M.D.

It's Great To Have A God How Cares by Meg Woodson

Quiet Moments from the Salesian Collection

Poems To Cherish from the Salesian Collection

Five Equations That Changed The World by Michael Guillen, Ph. D